Enneagram Business

How to Understand Your Personality Type Better
So You Can Use It to Your Advantage

(The Advanced Guide to Build Healthy
Relationships)

Casey Plummer

Published by Knowledge Icons

Casey Plummer

All Rights Reserved

Enneagram Business: How to Understand Your Personality Type Better So You Can Use It to Your Advantage (The Advanced Guide to Build Healthy Relationships)

ISBN 978-1-990084-58-4

All rights reserved. No part of this guide may be reproduced in any form without permission in writing from the publisher except in the case of brief quotations embodied in critical articles or reviews.

Legal & Disclaimer

The information contained in this book is not designed to replace or take the place of any form of medicine or professional medical advice. The information in this book has been provided for educational and entertainment purposes only.

The information contained in this book has been compiled from sources deemed reliable, and it is accurate to the best of the Author's knowledge; however, the Author cannot guarantee its accuracy and validity and cannot be held liable for any errors or omissions. Changes are periodically made to this book. You must consult your doctor or get professional medical advice before using any of the suggested remedies, techniques, or information in this book.

Upon using the information contained in this book, you agree to hold harmless the Author from and against any damages, costs, and expenses, including any legal fees potentially resulting from the application of any of the information provided by this guide. This disclaimer applies to any damages or injury caused by the use and application, whether directly or indirectly, of any advice or information presented, whether for breach of contract, tort, negligence, personal injury, criminal intent, or under any other cause of action.

You agree to accept all risks of using the information presented inside this book. You need to consult a professional medical practitioner in order to ensure you are both able and healthy enough to participate in this program.

Table of Contents

INTRODUCTION 1

CHAPTER 1: WHAT IS ENNEAGRAM? 3

CHAPTER 2: WHAT IS ENNEAGRAM USED FOR? 11

CHAPTER 3: UNDERSTANDING THE UNDERLYING PRINCIPLES OF THE ENNEAGRAM 25

CHAPTER 4: THE ENNEAGRAM PERSONALITY TYPE 2 - THE HELPER 41

CHAPTER 5: THE ACHIEVER SUBTYPES 54

CHAPTER 6: WHAT IS YOUR ENNEAGRAM PERSONALITY TYPE? 57

CHAPTER 7: ENNEAGRAM IN LOVE 64

CHAPTER 8: APPLYING WHAT YOU'VE LEARNED 78

CHAPTER 9: THE THREE AMIGOS 102

CHAPTER 10: THE BENEFITS OF REALLY KNOWING WHO YOU ARE 107

CHAPTER 11: IMPORTANT FOLKS AND WRITTEN RECORDS 117

CHAPTER 12: THE HELPER 123

CHAPTER 13: TYPE FOUR: THE UNIQUE CAREGIVER 129

CHAPTER 14: TYPE TWO PERSONALITY 153

CHAPTER 15: TYPE 1 AND 2 CHARACTERISTICS 167

CHAPTER 16: TYPE FIVE– THE INVESTIGATOR 173

CHAPTER 17: ENNEAGRAM AND RELATIONSHIPS WITH OTHER PEOPLE 179

CHAPTER 18: THE UNBALANCED ENNEAGRAM 184

CONCLUSION 189

Introduction

The Enneagram gives many perspectives on the nature of the ego. Some of the Enneagram's authors/researchers offer clear "health levels" that behaviorally define the general nature of an ego answer as they move in and out of the trance. Such rates of health provide a very simple barometer for self-development learners, where they are "at" as a result of a particular type of Enneagram in each case.

"To be productive and effective, your working lives must represent your true self and the power you already have." When you grew up, who do you want to be? Do you do what that childhood dream career would have been like now? While we can't all be ballerinas or astronauts, we can all find and create lives that make us happy. We can all choose professions that suit who we are at heart and are profoundly meaningful and productive.

The Enneagram is a complex personality assessment system that enables us to enhance our interaction with others dramatically. When you can understand another person's personality type, you know the motivation and find it easier to understand and accept them. They will also know what works for them and can formulate the words accordingly.

Chapter 1: What Is Enneagram?

Enneagram as a concept is all about individual differences that are deeply rooted in what motivates that individual, rather than what others perceive of him/her. Enneagram looks at the distinctions and variations in each type or group. The groups that are physically up and doing and those that are mentally active or those that love to socialize are all considered by enneagram. Some types love people to be drawn to them, while some others usually take their destiny into their own hands by going out of their ways to introduce themselves to others. In enneagram, each type is considered unique. What the enneagram does is to look at their strengths and weaknesses, for example their deepest desires or their deepest fears, are all shared and analyzed. This, in the long run, helps in categorizing them and helps in making them be able to work on their weaknesses, using those weaknesses into their advantages and consolidate their strengths. It is also up to them to use those strengths to their advantage and get better in every aspect of their life.

Now let us look at the dictionary definitions. According to Merriam Webster (2019), enneagram (any-a-gram) is a regular geometric figure with nine points: the figure inscribed within a regular nine-sided polygon. It is also a system of classifying personality types that are solely based on a nine-pointed star-like figure inscribed within a circle in which each of the nine points represents a personality type and its psychological motivations (such as the need to be right or helpful) influencing a person's emotions, attitudes, and behavior.

The Enneagram "Self-knowledge is tied with inner work, which is both demanding and painful. Many changes occur amid birth pangs. It takes courage to operate in those kinds of paths. Many people avoid the path of self-knowledge and illumination because they are afraid of being lost on their way to understand themselves or on their paths to discover themselves and become a better person through the new personality.

The etymology and development of the concept of enneagram of personality are somehow issues of dispute, and it can be said to be controversial. Many scholars have shown that some ideas to the enneagram of individual personality can be found in the books of many earlier writers and religious scholars who had worked passionately on the concept. The first thing in enneagram is what can be said to be self-love or love of self which is widely known as philautia; after this one, there are other eight personality types or groups. In addition to the commonly identified eight distinct thoughts or personalities, some scholars had also established some useful personality types, classes or groups which can be said to be stemmed from different beliefs and behaviors of every individual.

A scholar known as G.I. Gurdjieff who extensively worked on enneagram is the person that is credited with popularizing the enneagram of personality figure which is commonly known. However, he failed to develop the nine signs of enneagram of personality types that are duly linked with the enneagram. On the other hand, Oscar Ichazo is generally known and taken as the leading developer of the current enneagram of personality that is stemmed from many of Icaza's teachings. For instance, those that were derived on virtues, ego-fixations, passions, belief, holy ideas, and concept of self. This Bolivian-born scholar known as Oscar Ichazo started teaching programs of self-help self-belief, personality upgrade and self-development in the 1950s. His teaching, which was called protoanalysis which some scholars later referred to as photo analysis. In that teaching, he used the enneagram figure, in addition to many other ideas and symbols to buttress his points and to make it clear to his students. Ichazo was the founder of the Arica

Institute that was primarily founded and sited in Chile before it was later moved to the United States of America. He was the first to develop the word that is now widely known as the Enneagram of Personality.

On the other hand, Naranjo Claudio who was not a Bolivian but a known Chilean psychiatrist was the first person to learn the concept of the Enneagram of Personality from the great teacher Ichazo during the time when nobody was really interested in the concept. The course was organized in Arica, Chile, for many people but Claudio was the first person to learn the course and understand it fully. After that encounter, Claudio then started to develop, propagate, and teach his understanding of the concept of enneagram when he got back to the United States. All this happened in the early 1970s in the United States. Claudio started influencing other people including some notable personalities in the society especially the Jesuit priests who embraced and used the concept of enneagram in the teaching of Christian spirituality at the seminaries and churches. However, it's a great pity and so disheartened that Ichazo decided to disown his student, Naranjo and some other teachers who learned from him on what he felt were crass misinterpretations and wrong uses of the concept of the Enneagram of Personality. Also between Naranjo's early disciples, there are diverging understandings and opinions of the Enneagram of Personality theory. Many other great authors, especially Richard Rohr, Helen Palmer, Elizabeth Wagele, and Don Richard Riso, also started writing and publishing different opinions and diverse views that are widely read in the 80s and 90s. These views were on the Enneagram of Personality.

The enneagram figure is usually made of three distinct parts which is a circle, then an inner triangle that duly connects 3-6-9 and a very irregular hexagonal figure that can be said to be "periodic figure" that links 1-4-2-8-5-7 together. According to the beliefs of esoteric ideology, religious views, and traditions, the circle is said to symbolize unity, while the inner triangle stands for the "law or rule of three." And lastly, the hexagon, which is the third stands for the "law of seven." This is because all the 1-4-2-8-5-7-1 is the recurrent decimal created when one divides one by seven in base 10 and not in binary arithmetic. These three factors make up the known enneagram of personality figure.

Instinctual subtypes

Each of the temperament is sometimes understood as having 3 "instinctual subtypes." These subtypes square measure believed to be shaped in line with that one amongst 3 instinctual energies of an individual is dominantly developed and expressed.

The instinctual energies square measure typically referred to as "self-preservation," "sexual relationship" (known as "intimacy" also known as "one-to-one") or "social." On the instinctual operational level, people may internally stress and externally express the need to protect themselves (self-preservation), to link up with important people or partners (sexual), or to get along or achieve teams (social). From this view, there are twenty-seven different personality patterns, that is just because members belonging to each of the nine types also express themselves as being one of the nine subtypes. Well another view to the subtypes can be said to have three distinct clusters of instinctual behavior that lead to increased likelihood of survival (and that is the "preserving" domain), increased acquired skill in navigating the social environment (the "navigating" domain) and increased probability of fruitful success (the "transmitting" domain). From this understanding, the subtypes reflect individual differences in the presence of these three separate clusters of instincts.

It is believed many people perform all the mentioned varieties (the three instincts) of instinctual energies; however, one might dominate. According to some theorists, another instinct may also be well-developed and the third often less developed.

Chapter 2: What Is Enneagram Used For?

Often, when things seem uncertain it can be helpful to look inside oneself. For decades, people have been using personality tests in an attempt to organize the multitudes contained within them. The Myers-Briggs test, arguably the most well-known, places you into four categories based on self-reported traits and behaviors.

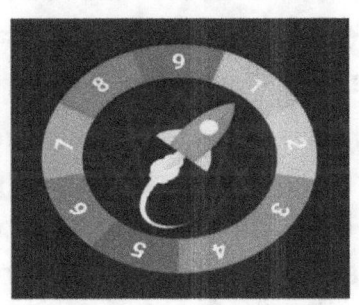

But a perhaps more comprehensive test may just give the standby a run for its money. The Enneagram Test is a modern take on a test originally created by a man named Oscar Ichazo. But what is the Enneagram test used for? According to the contemporary Enneagram Institute, at its inception, the test was used "as a way of examining specifics about the structure of the human soul and particularly about the ways in which the actual soul qualities of Essence become distorted, or contracted into states of ego." Further, the Enneagram originally "drew upon a recurrent theme in Western mystical and philosophical traditions - the idea of nine divine forms." These nine divine forms would become the basic pillars of the assessment.

Rather than having eight categories like the Myers-Briggs test, the Enneagram one has nine basic types and 27 subtypes. The basic categories, in descending order, are the reformer, the helper, the achiever, the individualist, the investigator, the loyalist, the enthusiast, the challenger, and the peacemaker. Once one completes the test, they find out their top three types (for example, mine are peacemaker, individualist, and loyalist). The results are displayed in a geometric prism-looking figure - a unique aspect of the test. Per the Enneagram Institute, the intent of the test is to, "help us to see ourselves at a deeper, more objective level and can be of invaluable assistance on our path to self-knowledge."

If you are on the path to self-awareness, maybe the Enneagram can give you a nudge in the right direction.

Before you can use the full Enneagram to fully dissect your personality, the best place to start is with this most basic version of the test. Within just a few minutes, it will give you the top three categories where you belong.

The coolest part about the Enneagram Test is just how much the placements allow you to do.

Where other tests may exclusively give you insight into how you think and behave, the Enneagram test may also give you guidance in your relationships. With 81 possible relationship combinations between the categories, there is a lot of behavior to analyze. Of course, just as the Enneagram Institute says, no two members of any given category are inherently destined for greatness or doomed. But, by taking the test, your partner and you may gain more insight into how you deal with conflict or how you can better collaborate.

The test is also utilized by many businesses to help employees determine the ways in which they will be most productive. In the upan-coming field of industrial and organizational psychology, Enneagram is just one example of a personality assessment used to help members of a professional team maximize their productive potentials. I took a version of the test during a group dynamics class I was enrolled in while studying psychology in college.

Naturally, the complexities of a human being's personality and the nuances of their behavior cannot be completely reduced to the categories of one simple test. You should view these assessments as a tool for learning more about yourself but not allow the results to make you act in ways with which you are uncomfortable.

Though, I do have to say, from a personal standpoint the basic Enneagram test sized me up with a surprising level of accuracy in the mere minutes it took to complete. I bet it would do the same for you.

BENEFITS OF ENNEAGRAM

The Enneagram is the rage, but most people don't know how to use it.

We coach pastors, leaders, and church groups in their personal growth and ministry effectiveness and the Enneagram is the best personality assessment tool we've seen. That's why we're doing a whole series of podcasts and blogs on its spiritual and psychological benefits.

Here are seven benefits of the Enneagram that most people miss:

1. Appreciating God's Presence

Many Enneagram teachers focus on spirituality, but not on our relationship with Christ. Sadly, even some Christian speakers do this. One of the talks we give is "The Nine Faces of Christ in the Enneagram." Using examples from the Gospels, we show how Jesus embodies each personality type in its perfection.

The primary reason to learn any personality system is to grow in our love for the Lord Jesus and learn from him how to better serve God with our lives.

2. Soul Awareness

At social gatherings, we may like to talk about differences in personality preferences and characteristics. That's fun and you can do that with the Enneagram, but it's just scratching the surface.

The theory of the Enneagram is that our personality has been malformed by sin, pain, stress, and defense mechanisms. We are bent away from God's loving presence. We have come up with our own self-help solution for life and it's not working. We don't see what we're doing and are stuck in destructive habits.

By relying on the Spirit of Jesus through the ancient wisdom of the Enneagram, we can grow in God's grace. For each type, there are levels of healthy and unhealthy.

3. Learning Your Basic Emotional Posture

Every type denies its core emotional problem with anger, shame, or anxiety. Even if you have healthy self-awareness of your feelings, often you're probably not in touch with your core emotion or your underlying sadness over losses and deficits you've experienced.

Being able to put your feelings into words and receive empathy improves your relationships and productivity. It invigorates your experience of God's loving presence and wisdom.

4. Godly Sorrow for Your Sin Pattern

The origins of the Enneagram go back to Evagrius, a Christian monk in the 4th Century who identified the deadly sins in human nature. The Enneagram unpacks nine root sins which form nine personality types. We need God's forgiveness, grace, and power through faith in Christ to be healed of our destructive patterns and be transformed into the image of Jesus.

5. Calming Your Reaction to Stress

When you know your type, the Enneagram predicts how you'll react to stress. In difficult situations, we all have an unconscious habit of incorporating another number's weaknesses. Once we become aware of this, we can then make better choices to stay tuned into God's loving presence.

6. Appreciating Your Growth Opportunity

The Enneagram also recommends a path of growth for you by identifying another type's "face of Christ" that you especially need to learn from. Incorporating the strengths of this type is a way of relying on God's grace to be your best self.

7. Empathy for Other People

We have to be careful with personality typing, especially with the power of the Enneagram. It's hurtful if we use our knowledge to judge people or tell them what their type is. It's better to encourage them to discover their type by "trying on" a few types until they find the one that best fits.

If we use the Enneagram in a Christ-like way, then we offer empathy and grace to other people in their type.

WHAT IS DIFFERENT ABOUT THE ENNEAGRAM?

We can do lots of tests based on our external behavior (shy/outgoing, creative/analytical, etc.) and they are fine but we a) don't really learn anything new about ourselves, and b) have different results depending on who we are with or how we feel. For example, you may be more aggressive and confident at home then you are at work.

The Enneagram doesn't slot you into a box or color. Sure, you get a number but the personality typing looks deeper. It is based on your motives, fears, and desires – all which are demonstrated by various behaviors depending on how 'healthy/secure' you are. It looks at the sum of which you are – all the blind spots and 'bad habits' we have when feeling insecure. It also looks at our strengths and unique abilities when we are feeling secure in who we are.

A Brief Overview of the Nine Types

Type One – The Perfectionist/The Reformer

Motivated by the desire to 'be good', they need to live life 'the right way'.

Healthy: ethical, reliable, productive

Unhealthy: judgmental, dogmatic, unrealistic expectations

Type Two – The Helper

Motivated by the need to be needed, they need to feel they are lovable and valuable.

Healthy: loving, generous, enthusiastic

Unhealthy: martyr, over-accommodating, indirect

Type Three – The Achiever/The Performer

Motivated by the need to be successful, they believe that their value lies in their achievements.

Healthy: optimist, practical, efficient

Unhealthy: narcissistic, workaholic, deceptive

Type Four – The Individualist/The Romantic/The Creative

Motivated by the need to be themselves, they need to understand their feelings and be understood.

Healthy: warm, compassionate, introspective

Unhealthy: depressed, self-conscious, guilt-ridden

Type Five – The Observer/The Investigator

They are motivated by the need to be capable, self-sufficient, and to know everything.

Healthy: analytical, wise, objective

Unhealthy: arrogant, distant, and critical

Type Six – The Questioner/The Skeptic/The Loyalist

Motivated by the need to have support, they need security.

Healthy: loyal, responsible, caring

Unhealthy: paranoid, controlling, rigid

Type Seven – The Enthusiast/The Adventurer

They are motivated by the need to be content, be happy, and avoid suffering.

Healthy: fun, spontaneous, confident

Unhealthy: rebellious, impulsive, and self-destructive

Type Eight – The Asserter/The Challenger/The Maverick

They are motivated by the need to protect themselves, to be selfreliant, strong and independent.

Healthy: direct, earthy, loyal, advocate for others

Unhealthy: controlling, skeptical, domineering, rebellious

Type Nine – The Peacemaker

They are motivated by the need to keep the peace and avoid conflict.

Healthy: diplomatic, open, calming

Unhealthy: stubborn, apathetic, and judgmental

How We Take on Traits of Other Types

We all have a basic personality type (our number) but we also have personality components of the types beside us (called our wings). Sometimes, we are leaning more toward one side than the other. So, if you are a Type 2 (the helper) you also have traits of either a Type 1 (the perfectionist) or Type 3 (the achiever).

Enneagram, ennea, enneatype, personality, personality types, personality test, self-awareness, self-growth, self-help, introspection.

Then, there are the lines that connect each type to two others. One line is your 'Direction of Integration'. When you are healthy and undergoing positive growth, you will pick up the positive traits of this other type. So, when a Type 2 is healthy, they take on the healthy qualities of Type 4 (the creative). The opposite is called 'Direction of Disintegration'. When you are experiencing stress, you will pick up the negative traits of this type. For instance, Type 6 (the loyalist) will pick up the unhealthy traits of Type 3 (the achiever).

L

Chapter 3: Understanding The Underlying Principles Of The Enneagram

Chances are you've already heard comments from numerous experts on the Enneagram. As you've already gathered, it is a symbol shrouded in mystical significance and the meaning and its different elements is not always clearly understood. This makes it difficult for some to embrace the idea; the lack of a direct explanation of the whole process often leaves some suspicious and wary, feeling that they may be entering a world of occultism.

For many, the occult is exactly what they think of when looking at the Enneagram symbol. Our minds automatically go there because it so closely resembles the pentagram, which is directly connected to modern occultism. This makes many pull back out of fear that they are getting involved in something dangerously mysterious and dark. However, by examining the symbol exclusive of any preconceived notions and clearing your mind from those ideas people tend to automatically associate with it, we begin to see some similarities that we can find in other more acceptable beliefs of our society.

It's a natural part of who we are to want to know more about the origins of anything we get involved in, and while the explanation of the symbol itself can sometimes seem vague and obscure, we have been able to uncover enough to unlock the true meaning of the Enneagram symbol. It may take a little digging to find it behind the different elements, but it will be well worth your while to do so.

However, it is very important to point out that the Enneagram we use today has changed a bit from its original purpose. One of the best ways to decipher it is by starting with the human mind. It is a natural tendency for our human brains to view images and break them down into different categories. Nothing fancy, it's just what the human brain is designed for. Since Gurdjieff is considered to be the father of the modern Enneagram, many will automatically associate the modern Enneagram with his symbol. Gurdjieff's teachings leaned heavily on the metaphysical - a means of organizing natural principles and using them to explain how the universe actually works.

There were three basic principles of Gurdjieff's metaphysical theory, all utilizing the Enneagram symbol. THE LAW OF SEVEN, UNITY, AND THE LAW OF THREE.

The Law of Seven: this law focused on the constant vibrations we all have around us. It is a little different from the Newtonian physics we have come to understand from modern science. Rather than what we've been taught - an object in motion stays in motion, the Law of Seven sees the world as a series of vibrations. According to this law, each object in motion must pass through seven separate stages before it comes to a stop. This means that the energy is not evenly spent but is instead, lost at very specific points before it can receive an additional infusion of energy to continue along its path.

His theory was based on the seven note musical octave with the idea that in nature, once something is in motion, that motion cannot be sustained forever. No matter what it is, it must deviate or change at specific intervals. As you go through a musical scale, for example, as the energy vibrations increase or decrease, the consistent rate naturally changes at certain points. With music, the points have been identified as the mi/fa point, and the si/do point. So in an octave of do re mi fa, so la ti do. The intervals where vibrations change would be between the mi and the fa at one point, and the si and the do at another point.

Of course, there is a lot more to the theory of the Law of Seven that we won't go into here.

According to Gurdjieff, the energy that is spent in vibrations does not uniformly dissipate but instead is lost at very precise points where it can receive an extra impulse to keep it going along its path.

Unity: When you first look at the Enneagram symbol, your eyes will automatically recognize the circle first. This is the universal symbol of unity and infinity. It can also signify the oneness and eternal nature of a Supreme Being. To Gurdieff, the circle represented two different forms of thinking. First, everything in the universe has a place, everything belongs with no exclusions. And secondly, the symbol was used to encourage a panoramic and more receptive awareness of the whole picture. This is done without judgment or labeling of anything as either good or bad. Anyone who can do this is able therefore to see the world in its true state and not be influenced by prejudices and personal preferences.

The Law of Three or the Triangle: This law represents the union of three fundamental things. First and foremost, the Supreme

Being of the universe (God) determines its nature and structure. Secondly, its organizing principle, and finally - the power he has to pull it all together. All three of these elements are key to understanding Gurdjieff's teachings of the Law of Three.

It is clear that Gurdjieff's teachings were extremely complex and detailed but understanding just these basic facts is key to being able to grasp the true purpose of the symbol. As human beings, we have always been in a sort of quandary. On the one hand, we are always in search of our own individuality, but on the other hand, we have a powerful, inbred need to belong to something bigger than ourselves. While the western world learned more towards seeing the individual to the point where nearly everything became disconnected, the eastern world strived for community and connectivity almost to the complete obliteration of the individual.

When you see the world with more importance placed on connections, the price you pay is a loss of human dignity, which is sacrificed for the sake of the whole. On the other hand, when too much importance is placed on the individual, the cost is the infringement on the rights of others. Therefore, the ability to create a balance between the two is essential and having the Spiritual Being holding it all together is key. With a Supreme Being, both unity and diversity can have an equal part in our lives, and we learn to live for both ourselves and for others.

While the ancient history of this symbol may seem vague and elusive, our modern understanding can offer us an even clearer meaning. The more we learn about it, the more we can dispel the fears of its dark and mysterious origins. Today, the symbol is used primarily as a schematic on a number of different personalities.

While the symbol we use today is not exactly the same as the symbol that he used (it has been refined over the decades to be more applicable to the world's society of today.) It has many practical applications once you begin to break it down. There are many different ideas as to how to use the symbol. With so many different personalities it is difficult at a glance to know where you actually fit on the personality spectrum. However, by the time you finish reading this book, you will have some very keen insight into the wisdom of the Enneagram so you can know exactly where you fit in the whole scheme of things.

Today's Enneagram

As we've already pointed out, the structure of the Enneagram is simply a circle with numbers and lines contained within it. Each of these numbers, circles, and lines can be analyzed and viewed from totally different aspects. In the basic Enneagram symbol, you'll first see a circle with numbers from one through nine around the perimeter in much the same way that the numbers go around a clock.

At first glance, the idea of a circle with numbered lines doesn't mean very much. At least, not until you begin to learn what each of these markings actually means. In the basic Enneagram symbol, the circle is a symbol of unity. The nine personality types are all equidistant from each other showing that they are all equal to one another. No single personality has more influence or power over any other. In essence, we all start on the same equal footing.

If you look closely, you will notice an inner triangle formed by connecting the points at the numbers three, six, and nine. This triangle represents a powerful and dynamic interaction of three different forces.

The Circle: You will see that there are nine different points spaced out around the circumference of the circle. We already understand that the circle is a representation of unity and the nine points are all equidistant from one another. This shows that each personality is equal but still connected to the others.

The Triangle: If you look closely, you will see an inner triangle that connects the three points at three, six, and nine. This represents the dynamic interaction of three very powerful forces. If you were to take two opposites, for example, the connecting force between the two would be some form of middle ground or a blend of each of the polar opposites. Here, three Enneagram Clusters are connected together by the triangle.

Hexad: If you were to look even closer, you would also see an irregular figure that connects all of the other six points. This part of the symbol represents the dynamic change we must all go through. As you will learn later, everyone has their own dominant personality, but it is not in control all the time. We are all constantly switching from one personality to another, each one represented by the Hexad, which connects them all together.

The Numbers: The nine numbers around the circumference represent the nine different personality types. Each type comes with its own seed of motivation that is responsible for triggering certain behaviors. While we all have a mixture of different personality types, we still have a primary or a stronger Enneagram type, which is responsible for our personal views on life, the actions we take, and how we respond to the world around us.

THE ARROWS: What you may not readily see in some Enneagram symbols are the arrows. However, if you see one with arrow tips at the ends of the lines, you'll notice that they follow a very exact structure that shows just how people shift personalities under varying circumstances. When you are under stress, confident, or achieving a personal level of growth, your behaviors will automatically and instinctively shift from one personality to another within your Cluster. We will move along those connecting paths following the directions of the arrows.

Arrows moving backward represent your stress personality, which is your automatic way of separating yourself from your usual behavior and protecting yourself from emotional damage. When some people face severe stress, they could switch to this stress point and remain there for days, weeks, months, and sometimes even years before they feel safe enough to return to their dominant personality.

On the other hand, forward pointing arrows travel a path to a more secure place that will permit you to perform out safer behaviors. When you are at your security point, you are usually in familiar surroundings with people you can trust. When you are healthy, you might make a move to your Integration Point. This is where you blend together qualities that will create a delicate balance between confidence and structure. If you're looking to grow, it is important that you embrace these Security Points and follow those healthy behaviors applying them in your life.

By now, you've probably already begun to identify with a particular Personality Type. I fact, you've probably narrowed it down to several. If you're interested in pinpointing exactly which Personality Type you are, there are several resources you can find online that can help you. Some of them are free but those worth their salt will cost you a little bit of money to take the test. However, the benefits you can gain from this knowledge can be very valuable to you and can help you to improve your life in many different ways. We'll include a list of those towards the end of the book.

It is easy to see why so many people are intrigued by The Enneagram and what it can mean for them. It is a tool that gives you the ability to look at your own life and see it for what it really is. It provides the right frame for looking inside and identifying specific patterns that have been influencing your every decision since birth.

With this increased knowledge about yourself, you can feel empowered to venture off into different territories that reach outside of your personal comfort zone. As you do, your life's purpose will become clearer and your course in life, your destiny will unfold before you. Learning your Enneagram personality is just as much a spiritual journey as it is a psychological one, but if you take it with an open mind, it is possible for you to achieve greater intelligence about the human mind and discover your personal calling. However, it will require you to look deeper below the surface at what's inside for you to do so.

The Iceberg

Humans are highly complex creatures and are made up of many different elements. While we all have the same components, it is the unique combination of those elements that make us individuals. Your personality is made up of a delicate composite of several elements that reflect not just your inner feelings and experiences but also shows up in how you express yourself and interact with those around you. Each element has its own role to play in building up the personality that exists in you.

It has often been described as an iceberg. While the iceberg is massive in size, what you see above the surface of the water are simply those elements that you are consciously aware of. It is the part of our personality that we allow others to see. However, the vast majority of what makes us who we are is what lies beneath the surface, the part of us that either we are not aware of or the part that we will try desperately to hide from those in our lives.

These hidden elements are the very things that drive us to perform certain behaviors. To put it more simply, those hidden parts of our personality can be described as those things that we feel while those things that are visible to our naked eye could be viewed as the elements that inform us and we consciously react to. Together these all encourage our behavior and give us the motivation to do the things we do.

In order for the Enneagram to be most effective and beneficial for us, we must address what is both above and below the line. The combination is what provides us with the insight and the wisdom to make the changes we may feel we need to improve.

Chapter 4: The Enneagram Personality

Type 2 - The Helper

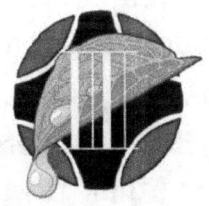

This Enneagram personality type is also called The Giver. This personality type feels that their worth comes from being helpful to others. They are very aware of the needs of others and feel that love is the highest ideal. These people tend to be extroverts and are very socially active because giving to others is their reason for being. If you know someone who always remembers someone else's birthday or goes out of their way to help others then this person is likely a type 2.

What Makes the Helper a Great Personality

THE HELPER IS EMPATHETIC. This personality type is deeply in tune with the needs of others as a result of being able to tune into the energy that other people give off. They often have that instinctive knowhow of when a person is in need of help and is of course, eager to help.

THE HELPER IS THOUGHTFUL OF THE NEEDS OF OTHERS. This person is deeply focused in making their relationships with other people work and work tirelessly to support and love the people they develop these relationships with. As a result, most people think of them in a positive way.

THE HELPER IS NURTURING AND GENEROUS. This person does not hesitate to give the shirt off their backs or lend a shoulder to cry on. This person is a caring personality who loves to share.

THE HELPER PRACTICES GENUINE SELF-SACRIFICE. This person is so deeply in tune with the needs of others that they often give preference to the needs of others rather than their own needs.

The Deadly Sins of the Helper

THE HELPER CAN BE INTRUSIVE. Type 2s are deeply emotional and are people who spend a great deal of time developing their personal relationships. Due to the amount of time and energy that they spend, they often expect to be appreciated for their efforts and much of their self-image revolves around how helpful they are to other people. These people need to be needed by others and their love is not entirely without ulterior motive. They often develop a sense of entitlement due to the energy that they expend helping others and feel that they have earned the right to be intrusive if others do not readily cooperate in the way they view things.

THE HELPER CAN BE POSSESSIVE. These people are possessive of the relationships that they have and feel betrayed if the people they have relationships with turn to other people for help instead of them.

THE HELPER CAN BE MANIPULATIVE. As a result of feeling that they are always right in their need to help others and that their way of helping is the best way, this personality type can become quite conniving in the way that they approach dealing with other people. They feel entirely justified in their actions because they feel that they have earned the right because their intentions of being helpful are good. If type 2s do not get their way, they can become hysterical, irrational, and sometimes abusive.

THE HELPER CAN BE SELF-NEGLECTIVE. Due to the fact that they spend most of their time helping other people, they often forget to tend to their own emotional, physical, spiritual, and mental needs. That attention is most often focused on other people and causes them to lose sight of themselves and their own needs. This often leads to burnout. Therefore type 2s need to learn to service themselves as well as others so that they can remain balanced and healthy in all ways.

THE HELPER CAN HAVE LOW SELF-ESTEEM. As a result of the focus on other people, Helpers can feel a deflated self of self-worth depending on the approval of others.

How Helpers Relate to Other Personality Types

Helpers vs. Type 1s

Please see Chapter 2: How Reformers Relate to Other Personality Types: Reformers vs. Type 1s.

Helpers vs. Type 3s

Both of these personality types are driven by their emotions even though it is not as obvious with type 3s. They both love attention and have a desire to be loved. As a result, both are people-oriented and love being in the spotlight. This can make a great relationship if the two personality types nurture each other's needs. Unfortunately, a pairing such as this can lead to jealousy and possessiveness because neither type wants to take second place or to let the other shine brighter than them.

Helpers vs. Type 4s

These two can make a warm and affectionate romantic couple since they are both seeking warmth and a genuine connection with someone else. Unfortunately, these two personality types hardly ever form romantic relationships because they can both be too emotional and place too many demands on each other. They more often make great friends and colleagues.

Helpers vs. Type 5s

Type 2s and 5s are complete opposites in the way that they think, what they believe is important in life, and how they approach relationships. When they do form lasting relationships, they are the epiphany of opposites attract. Because type 5s are emotionally distant creatures, Helpers often seen them as a challenge. When a healthy relationship blooms, Helpers bring warmth and ease to the relationship while type 5s bring stability and objectivity. Conflict may arise with the boundaries that these two personality types set for each other and how respectful they are toward each other. Because type 5s are so unresponsive to emotional stimuli, type 2s can become frustrated and hurt by this lack of response. This can trigger anxiety and the type 2's intrusive, manipulative nature.

Helpers vs. Type 6s

Both these personality types take responsibilities in a relationship very seriously. They differ in their approaches. Helpers focus on building intimacy and positivity between the two while the Loyalist focuses on building stability and trust. Because these two personality types are both so responsible, they easily share duties in a relationship. Type 6s value the warmth and generosity that type 2s bring to the table while type 2s value the steadfastness, modesty, and hard-working nature of type 6s. The main problem that these two personality types face in their relationships are issues of control and authority. Types 6s can feel pressure by type 2s to be more decisive. Their help and advice can be perceived as intrusive. This undermines the type 6s self-confidence, and anxiety and resentment can arise in the relationship.

Helpers vs. Type 7s

These two personality types are similar in many ways such as being extroverted, high energy, their need to make others happy, and being positive. As a pair, these two can excel in their generosity and thoughtfulness toward other people. The issue may arise in the fact that type 2s always want to get closer while type 7s tend to want to wait to settle down. Type 7s do not like limiting their options and while they are capable of maintaining long-term relationships, they tend to hold off for as long as possible. Type 2s can even push them away with their need to hover and become intrusive.

Helpers vs. Type 8s

Both of these personality types are action-oriented, deeply feeling, and Protectors. They bring passion and vitality to the relationship. They help balance each other out. Type 2s are affectionate and appreciate the strength and practicality of type 8s while type 8s love their nurturing and caring qualities. These two work as a pair because their roles in a relationship are so clearly delineated. They are different in their value systems. Type 8s are practical, independent people while type 2s are more sentimental and become more attached. These two personality types normally find conflict in their different philosophies in life.

Helpers vs. Type 9s

Again, these two personality types are similar. They are both nurturing and love healing other people. They are both warm, kind, undemanding, and hospitable. As a pair, they project high energy and provide comfort together. Type 2s are constantly adding new people to the mix to help and this can give rise to stress and conflict. Type 9s prefer matter remain uncomplicated. When these two personality types find balance and make a relationship work, they are a very mellow and generous couple. Problems may arise because both of them prefer to take the backseat in controlling a relation but ultimately someone has to wear the pants. Taking control goes against the nature of both of these personality types. Also both types find it hard to express their feelings and easily grow discontent.

How The Help Can Improve His Or Her Life

Helpers can improve their lives by taking the time for introspection. This self-examination will allow them to get in touch with their own needs so that they can direct some of the energy that they use to tend to others inward.

The Helper can also benefit by letting someone else help them out for a change. This would bring balance to their relationships and help them see that give and take can exist in a healthy accord with each other. Actionable steps that the Helper can use to improve their life include:

- PRACTICING ROOT CHAKRA MEDITATION. This type of meditation helps improve mental stability so that the Helper can deal with their own needs. To do this, the meditation practitioner must let the tips of their thumb and index finger touch then concentrate on the root chakra at the point between the genitals and the anus while chanting.

- PRACTICING CROWN CHAKRA MEDITATION. This helps develop self-awareness and wisdom. To do this, the practitioner must put their hands on their stomach and let the ring fingers point up so that they touch at the tops. The next step is to cross the rest of the fingers, allowing the left thumb to sit underneath the right. Concentrate on the crown chakra at the top of your head while chanting.

- PRACTICING ACUPRESSURE. To reduce the effects of having too much emotion on the body, an acupressure practitioner can stimulate the point called P-7, which is located in the middle of the palm side of the wrist in the depression between the two tendons. Stimulating this acupressure point also helps diminish nervousness. The Helper can also be aided by the stimulation of the point ST-36 so that he or she can be more stable in dealing with his or her own needs. This point is located on the front of the leg just below the kneecap in the depression between the shin bone and the leg muscles.

Additionally, the Helper needs to:

- Understand that without first addressing their own needs, they cannot efficiently address the needs of other people.

- Become more conscious of their own motives when they decide to help others so that they help for the sake of helping rather than with an ulterior motive that will set them up for disappointment.

- Ask how a person may need help rather than assuming.

- Communicate their intentions to help before taking action and be willing to accept that a person does not need their help.

- Stop calling attention to the fact that he or she is being helpful and let kindness be its own reward.
- Learn to recognize the affection and love that others give even if they are not in the form that he or she would have perceived as best.
- Volunteer in community activities and homeless shelters where their giving nature will be much appreciated.
- Learn to accept the help of other people.

Chapter 5: The Achiever Subtypes

The three subtypes associated with the achiever are: security, charisma, and prestige. You can learn more about these subtypes and what they mean below.

Self-Preservation: Security

The achiever who is dominant in the security subtype will likely refrain from being too "flashy" about their strengths or achievements. They tend to dislike being seen as individuals who are too focused on their image, and instead would like to be recognized for their hard work and the excellence they achieve as a result of that hard work.

The security subtype of the achiever means that they are reliable, productive, and often very efficient at what they do. When they set their mind to something or give you their word, you can feel completely confident that they will do what they have promised to do. They always aspire to do the right thing.

The security-driven achiever desires to be self-sufficient and may find themselves living the lives of a workaholic as they use hard work as a means to get there.

One-on-One: Charisma

Achievers like to use their competitiveness as a way to support other people. They love seeing success in others, as they feel this is a sense of personal success as well, especially if they feel they contributed to the other person's success. If an achiever is dominant in the charismatic subtype, they may base their entire victory based off of the achievement of those around them. Thus, they become heavily invested in other people's triumph.

A charismatic achiever is known to compete for the affection and attention of other people, especially those who are closest to them. They may even find themselves suppressing their own feelings and needs as a way to make themselves appear more attractive to other people. This is so that they can avoid conflict and be seen as more "approachable" and enjoyable. They feel this is a great way for them to improve their likelihood of receiving the most attention and affection from their loved ones.

Social: Prestige

Because of their competitive nature, achievers tend to desire influence. They can be very skillful when it comes to reading situations and adjusting to the social norms of their environment. This makes it so that they can massively impact their influence. This makes them incredible when it comes to being in the spotlight, marketing their ideas, and sharing or promoting their accomplishments.

To the achiever who is dominant in the prestige subtype, they may find themselves needing to look good in front of others. They absolutely crave success, sometimes to the point of cutting corners and covering up failures so that they can appear even more successful. As long as the final outcome makes them and their team look good, the prestigious achiever will be happy.

Chapter 6: What Is Your Enneagram Personality Type?

There's nothing so invigorating as the minute that someone else "gets you." That feeling of quick acknowledgment and silent comprehension is finished enchantment. We know it with a few—possibly just a couple—yet the ones who hold that piece of us do as such for a lifetime.

This is actually the sort of feeling I felt the minute I found a character composing framework called The Enneagram and it changed the manner in which I approach sentiment for eternity.

The Enneagram depends on an old character composing framework and is separated into nine numbers and subdivided into three ternions. The groups of three speak to the head, the heart, and the gut, which are the three fundamental parts of the human mind. The uniqueness of the Enneagram in a wash of character composing frameworks is this: paying little heed to type, it goes up against pursuers with two pathways inside their essential or prevailing sort: The Direction of Integration, which clarifies how a sort is probably going to carry on when on a pathway of wellbeing and development, and The Direction of Disintegration, which clarifies how a specific kind is probably going to act under pressure and weight.

Enneagram types won't give you a horoscope perusing, your visionary sign, or the following spot to locate the ideal date (If as it were!). In any case, it holds interesting knowledge into the inclinations that keep us away from sound associations with ourselves as well as other people. All things considered, the more joyful, increasingly coordinated people we become, the more probable we will discover and support sound connections—particularly in those early periods of association.

Here are a couple of bits of knowledge for each sort:

TYPE ONE: The Perfectionist. Moral, devoted and solid, Ones are inspired by a longing to live the correct way, improve the world, and stay away from deficiency and fault.

Relationship update: Embrace suddenness and bliss by proposing an unconstrained date. Ease the heat off by discharging control of desires and results. The world won't self-destruct when you kick your heels back.

TYPE TWO: The Helper. Warm and sympathetic, twos are persuaded by a should be adored and required and are constantly caught up with becoming a close acquaintance with outsiders and supporting their interpersonal organizations.

Relationship update: Try not to be consumed by the necessities of your loved one and venture quickly to ask: "How's it hanging with you?" Fight the inclination to hop in and fix others' issues, regardless of whether you're great at it.

TYPE THREE: The Performer. Achievement arranged, picture cognizant and wired for efficiency, threes are driven by a need to prevail no matter what, and to maintain a strategic distance from disappointment.

Relationship update: Know that somebody's energy about you isn't constantly attached to your achievements. You have a great deal of profundity to offer. Be focused on making bona fide associations over driving with your vocation renown or economic wellbeing.

TYPE FOUR: The Romantic. Fours are huge in their inventiveness and articulation however are especially delicate to being misconstrued. They have propensities to be excessively sensational or stuck in their feelings.

Relationship update: Take supply of your feelings yet don't generally decide to go into them. Utilize your forces of observation to place yourself from your date's point of view and see things from their side of the table.

TYPE FIVE: The Observer. Diagnostic, confined and private, fives are inspired by a need to pick up information, ration vitality and disengage from the desires for other people so they can take part in scholarly interests.

Relationship update: Don't fear getting "pulled in" near to another. Your sentiments aren't a lot for another person to deal with. You have the stuff to be great at connections when you move from your head space to hearts space.

TYPE SIX: The Loyalist. Submitted, reasonable and competent, sixes are the most stressed of the considerable number of types because of their requirement for security and inborn suspiciousness of power. In any case, sixes at their best are especially ardent and steadfast companions.

Relationship update: Know that not every person has a "concealed motivation" and that it's sheltered to be hopeful temporarily. Utilize your capacity of fellowship and dependability to manufacture a reliable association with a date or significant other.

TYPE SEVEN: The Enthusiast. Fun, unconstrained and delight chasing, sevens are roused by a should be upbeat and social, having a lot of animating encounters however maintaining a strategic distance from torment.

Relationship update: Commitment isn't such an awful thing. Push back on your desire to escape and face what may be driving you to anxious yet shallow movement. You have such a great amount of intelligence to offer by staying grounded and focused.

TYPE EIGHT: The Challenger. Ordering, extreme and amazing, eights are searching for the closest victory. They are propelled by a requirement for control and can regularly be defenders of the dark horse.

Relationship update: Your capacity is in your demonstration of delicacy similarly as your solid character. Individuals can love and deal with the genuine you, in any event, when a touch of helplessness surfaces. In the event that you feel a tear entering discussion, don't keep it down.

TYPE NINE: The Peacemaker. Wonderful, laid back and pleasing, nines have the endowment of seeing any single issue from numerous points, yet experience difficulty standing up for themselves because of wants to keep the harmony, converge with someone else's lifestyle, and maintain a strategic distance from strife.

Relationship update: You needn't generally "come to get along". You have consent to voice a differentiating conclusion from your date's point of view, regardless of whether that makes you apprehensive. Feel free to step out!

The Enneagram character test is the initial step to discovering which of the nine-character profiles you fall under.

It's sort of unwinding to see your entire character enveloped with one basic word yet the cool thing about the Enneagram character test is, it's a model of interconnected character types, which means there's a tad bit of every one of them in each one of us.

When you've taken the Enneagram test, an entire universe of data opens up to you, remembering the ways for which you work, impart and even experience passionate feelings for.

Chapter 7: Enneagram In Love

When it comes to love, does compatibility matter? A standard line that almost all those who have ever gone through a breakup use is "in the end, we weren't compatible." Compatibility might sound quite vague, but it can mean a lot of things. It can mean any of the following things:

We used to annoy each other to the extent that we weren't fond of each other towards the end. We didn't share or respect each other's values. Our expectations didn't match. Our conflicts baffled our love for each other. We didn't know how to deal with our conflicts.

Compatibility can mean anything, and it differs from one person to the other. So, what exactly does being compatible mean? According to the dictionary, it denotes the ability to live in harmony without any conflicts. It is quite impossible to maintain a relationship that is devoid of all conflicts. Conflicts are common in all relationships in life, from your family, friends, to any romantic relationship. It is kind of surprising when you think about it, isn't it, that the person that we used to think the world of suddenly becomes someone who doesn't even seem like a friend anymore?

When a relationship ends, the feeling of sympathy that you feel towards the person seems to disappear altogether. If you want a long-term relationship to last, then there needs to be a balance between novelty and comfort. It is ironic when, at times, both familiarity and novelty become quite irritating in a relationship. We all know the story. A couple falls in love. She falls for him because he is fun to be around and caring like her father was, maybe steady and sensitive as well. He falls in love with her because she is caring and nurturing like his mother, and she seems to be up for an adventure. Well, that does sound like an ordinary couple, doesn't it? Yes, it is good initially. After a couple of months or maybe years though, they feel tricked. They feel that there was false advertising on both sides.

Where has her sense of adventure gone? Why has he become uncaring? Why don't they share the same interests anymore? She likes to shop and gossip, while he likes to play golf with his buddies. Oh my, where did that ideal relationship go? Where did their shared values go? They seem to be getting on each other's nerves for every little thing.

It is painful when the person you turned to for comfort seems like your persecutor. These frustrations are an indication of the direction in which you and your partner should grow. However, what is quite tragic is that instead of working on these problems like a team, most of us make it about our suffering. Therefore, we use the term "incompatible."

The first thing that you need to understand is that conflicts are inevitable. Fights are normal, and they are bound to happen. If you want your relationship to mature, then you should expect a couple of rows now and then. The more things you have in common with your partner, the less disturbing and persistent the conflicts will seem. If you share common views about upbringings, demographics, and even world-views, the conflicts won't look too distressing. It doesn't mean that you shouldn't have any differences in opinions. Everyone has different ideas, and the difference in views is what causes conflicts. Conflicts are healthy, and you must expect them. The one thing that you should focus on is resolving the disputes that come up. A conflict doesn't mean the end of a relationship.

In fact, it is an opportunity for the couple to understand each other better. Don't think of conflict as a feeling of friendship or the lack of conflicts. Maybe it is time to change the way we look at compatibility these days. Even when we don't feel the fondness for the other, there might still be some compatibility left. If you can interpret the reason for the dissatisfaction instead of making it about personal suffering, it might help.

There are different styles of conflict, and they can be categorized into four categories. The four styles of conflict are avoidant, validating, hostile, and volatile. The only couples who are in real trouble are the ones that fall into the hostile category. Everything else can be managed with a little mutual understanding.

The one question that bothers most of us is "did I pick the right person?" Well, how can we pick someone perfect, when we are flawed? No one is perfect and to expect perfection from others is foolhardy. You might be wondering where the

Enneagram fits in with all this. Well, have a little patience. There are different types of personalities, and each has its own good and bad traits. You need to understand that regardless of the type compatibility you share, relationships all boil down to how the partners deal with conflict.

There is no such thing as a perfect couple. If you still believe in that concept, you should give up on it. Instead, you should focus on different aspects of your relationship and try to make it better. According to the Enneagram, there are 45 possible combinations. For instance, One with a One, One with a Two, One with a Three, One with a Four, and so on. Some might wonder what a particular pairing works better than the rest. A type combination cannot predict the success of a relationship.

Every Enneagram type has specific imbalances in a relationship. A couple of common shortcomings are listed below. Remember that it isn't an exhaustive list. If you feel that you and your partner have any of these imbalances, then you can try to work things out slowly.

Type Ones tend to love control. They can be controlling and criticizing in a relationship to the extent that the other person can feel dejected. If you are a Type One, then don't try to micromanage things. Let go of a little control and trust your partner.

Type Twos are givers. It is in their nature to help others. However, if you are a Type Two and you ignore your needs for long, it will lead to resentment. Resentment can sour a relationship quicker than anything else. If you have specific expectations, it is best if you talk about them with your partner.

All Type Threes try to bypass their emotions. As a Type Three person, when you ignore your feelings, it will make you feel lonely and empty, even when there isn't a reason for you to feel so. If you feel something, discuss it with your partner.

Type Fours are individualists. As a Type Four person, it is good to retain your identity in a relationship, and you shouldn't give up on it. However, too much individualism can make your partner feel left out. Don't spend too much time mulling about what you feel, after all, you aren't the only one that feels things.

All Type Fives need to stop withdrawing themselves from their partners. It can make your partner feel anxious. Independence is good, but remember that you are a team. You cannot have a successful relationship if you both act as individual entities all the time.

Type Six personalities have issues with anxiety, so much so that others can feel tested and mistrusted. A Sixes doubts and unnecessary fears shouldn't be the reason for their partner's sleepless nights. If you're a Six, it is critical that you tell your partner about the things that trouble you.

Type Sevens love to multitask and spend a lot of time thinking about the future. However, Sevens, when you spend all your time thinking about a future that might or might not happen, you ignore your presence. Learn to live in the moment.

Type Eights don't like to feel vulnerable. Whenever they feel a slight vulnerability creeping in, they tend to shut others away. All you type Eight personalities, don't push your partner away. If you behave like they aren't wanted, they will soon assume that you don't need them.

Type Nines love harmony. They love peace more than anything. It means that they try to shy away from conflicts. Nines, you cannot ignore disputes all the time. If you want a healthy relationship, you need to learn to discuss things with your partner.

If you want a better relationship, then here are a couple of simple things that will help you along the way.

Hear

You need to make sure that you are both physically and mentally present when your partner is speaking to you. Let down your defenses and open your heart. You must try and understand your partner so that you can fulfill their needs. It's not verbal communication that you need to watch out for, but non-verbal communication as well. Notice whether your partner is angry, the expression in their eyes, body language, hand gestures, and tone of voice. It will help you understand what your partner is feeling. Your partner needs to reciprocate the same as well.

Empathize

Once you are confident that you understand what your partner is feeling, you need to pay attention towards the feelings that you have when you observe your partner. It is essential to search for the tender and the softer feelings towards your partner. Can you connect with your partner on a deeper level and feel pain when your partner is in pain? Can you be compassionate towards your partner and let your partner know the same? Your first instinct might be to offer advice or try and solve the problem when you know that your partner is in distress. Though your intentions are good, this comes across as being judgmental or even critical. Instead, the pure expression of compassion can soothe your partner's distress and calm them down as well. More than advice, this is what your partner might need most of the times.

Act

You will need not only to take action to deal with your partner's needs and concerns but will also have to show that you are willing to change. These actions needn't be anything elaborate; they can be something as simple as helping with chores around the house, calling your partner during the day because you miss them, and perhaps spending less money when you know your partner gets anxious about it. When your partner can see that you are taking the concerns they express seriously, your partner will feel valued and respected. It will initiate a positive cycle where your partner will appreciate you and you will understand your partner. You needn't be perfect; you do need to act in a manner that shows that you care and that you are trying to change.

Love

You need to feel and express your unconditional love towards your partner. You need to deliberately make some space in your life if you want to reconnect with your partner. Even if the recent interactions that you had with your partner left you feeling angry and distant, you need to make an effort if you want your marriage to survive. Think of all the good qualities that your partner has, the ones that made you love them initially. Go through your photo albums or think of those times when you felt that you had everything that you ever wished for and more. You need to find a way to not just forgive the mistakes you made but also the ones that your partner made, the errors that pushed you off track.

The feeling of love that you have towards your partner—what does it make you do? You might want to reach out and express your love towards your partner in a physical form or might want to do something special like taking them for a meal to their favorite restaurant or anything that you can think of. Your expression of love shouldn't depend on how your partner reacts, but it should be unconditional. If you think there's a particular issue that's holding you back from expressing your unconditional love, care, support, and trust towards your partner, then you need to take steps to get these issues sorted out.

Respect

Respect is critical when it comes to building a healthy relationship. You must make the effort of understanding and respecting all your partner's interests. Even if some things are not to your liking, you cannot ask them to quit it; this will not lead to a sustainable and lasting relationship. Your partner must reciprocate the respect, for the relationship to work out.

Empathy

Remember that there is no room for selfishness in a relationship and empathy takes center stage. Empathy refers to understanding your partner's point of view and providing comfort. If you showcase humanity and compassion, then your partner is sure to feel attracted to you and will reciprocate.

Trust

One of the most critical foundational stones of a healthy relationship is trust. Both you and your partner must trust each other and give one another enough room to make independent decisions. Interfering in each other's matters or lack of trust can all lead to cracks in the relationship. It can start off as a small complaint and become more prominent with time.

Loyalty

This one goes without saying. If you want your relationship to last and work out, then you must be loyal to your partner. It is in human nature to be tempted, but what is essential is having love and respect for your partner and doing right by them.

Chapter 8: Applying What You've Learned

The major advantage of knowing your own Enneatype is understanding how you should be interacting with other Types. Below you may find a helpful and concise guide. Please, remember that this is a very practical overview of potential interactions between the Enneatypes. If you wish to dive into the details behind each of these relationships, there are many good resources out there which can satisfy your curiosity. One good place to start is visit "The Enneagram Institute"

So let's get on with our relationships guide!

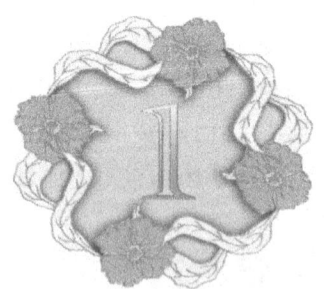

Type   One

Relationships

When a One interacts with another One, it may seem like that could be disastrous, but it can actually work out quite well considering how well their ideal align. However, Ones should be careful about getting into a never-ending improvement project.

A One matched with a Two may be quite complementary as well. A Reformer and a Helper tend to fill in each other's gaps quite well.

A One pair with a Three has the potential to be a very productive and idealistic relationship. Just be sure you are devoting as much energy inward as you are outward.

A relationship between a One and a Four can be a very free, easy-going and expressive one. Caution should be in order though, as a Four's tendency to act on emotion and feeling may clash with your logical reasoning.

Ones tend to also have a lot in common with Fives, with the primary difference being that Fives tend to have a strong focus on the abstract, while Ones are more practical. Therefore both should remember to remain open-minded to each other's ideas.

Even more similar, Ones and Sixes are so alike, they often misidentify as each other. Sixes may be a little bit quicker to emotion though, so One should remember to be patient.

Sevens are arguably the most complementary to Ones, in an "opposites attract" kind of way. While they balance each other out very well, a One must be aware that a Seven's idealism and free-spiritedness may at times come across as childish or undisciplined.

Eights potentially can be somewhat likeminded with Ones, with each being likely to be passionate about truth and justice. However, their differences tend to chip away at the relationship, so beware.

And when it comes to Nines, Ones tend to understand them very well, despite differences, and a Nine often has a tempering effect on a One. However, different approaches to stress and conflict may lead to imbalance.

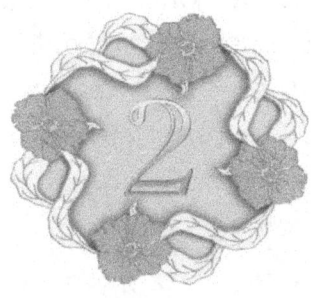

Type Two Relationships

Twos should value Ones for their complementary qualities, and similar goals and values. But be sure to keep the lines of communication open to avoid conflict.

A Two paired with another Two, obviously will be a warm and caring relationship. However, jealousy can very easily creep into such a pairing, even if it's a friendship or familial relationship.

Twos and Threes are both highly emotional, even though that's more apparent in Twos. However, what at first may appear to be common goals, may turn into points of serious stress and contention.

A Two and a Four may struggle to achieve intimacy at first, but once they do, it will be warm and passionate. Unspoken wants and misunderstood needs may make this pairing more appropriate friendship, although when it works, this can make for a very healthy romantic pairing.

Twos and Fives are certainly opposites, in terms of both thoughts and feelings. This can lead to intense attraction between them, and it can work rather well. Just be careful to have well-defined boundaries and strong communication.

Twos and Sixes tend to have very loyal and serious relationships. This can make for a strong foundation, but make sure to remember to bring joy and levity into the relationship.

Sevens on the surface may seem quite similar to Twos, and they are both certainly friendly, outgoing, sociable people. Differing long-term ideals and feelings of lack of space may lead to trouble though, so beware to keep communication free and open.

Twos and Eights don't seem very similar at all on the surface, but they can both have similar interiors. However, be aware and respectful of differing values.

Nines are helpers and nurturers just like Twos. However, this often leads to a relationship in which no one takes charge.

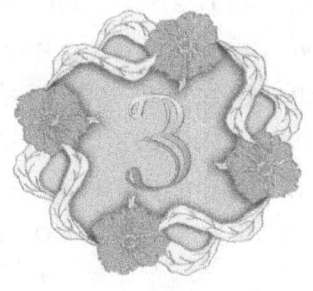

Type Three Relationships

A Three paired with a One is a very goal-oriented relationship, with only One-One or a Three-Three pairs being more so. Be careful of blind spots that may develop while you both have your eyes on the prize.

Three's and Two's can be a very fulfilling pairing. Three's should be aware that a Two's helpfulness may come across as possessiveness.

Fours tend to possess a number of qualities that Threes lack, and vice versa, so they make good compliments. But be careful of mutual low self-esteem dragging you down into a spiral of negativity.

Fives can bring a creative spark to a Three that may have been lacking otherwise, and you can expect to be seen as a very intelligent and successful relationship, although a mutual desire for excellence may lead to undue criticism of perceived weaknesses.

A Six paired with a Three is one we don't see terribly often, even though it may seem to make sense. It certainly can work, just be aware that you may end up possessing many of the same negative qualities.

A particularly complementary pairing, Threes and Seven's each bring their own energy to very similar qualities. But having that much energy and intensity in one pair could lead to a powder keg of volatility, so be sure to communicate through any potential issues.

Three and Eights are both the types of people who know what they want and will work hard to get it, so they can make for a very effective and goal-oriented pair. This is also the type of pair that could be prone to jealousy and competitiveness, so both will need to be able to handle that.

A Nine paired with a Three makes for a relatively common pair. Nines are supportive and encouraging, which can be very powerful in enhancing a Threes positive intrinsic qualities. Be careful with this pairing, however, to not become too entrenched in routines and the dopamine loop of positive feedback.

Type Four Relationships

Fours and Ones both can have a strong desire to create and build things, literally or figuratively. Both believe in self-expression and tend to be idealistic. But if those ideals aren't very closely aligned, they can find themselves drifting away from one another before too long.

A Four and Two pair will be very open and emotionally supportive, with both parties being warm and passionate. Because the tendencies of each partner though, be careful not to develop an unhealthy pattern of the Four needing to have constant problems for the Two to fix.

Fours generally tend to match rather well with Threes. They have complementary attributes that can keep that pair productive and healthy. It is possible though, for this pairing to develop issues of requiring each other's validation in too many, if not all areas.

Despite the moniker of Individualist, two Fours can make quite a good pair; each understands the other's desire for individuality. Be careful that the relationship doesn't become too self-serving though, which each half generally knowing exactly what they what to get out of a relationship.

Fours and Fives make for deep, complex pairings that can be very fulfilling. It's possible for an intimacy-independence imbalance to develop, though.

A Four and a Six tend to be naturally, if maybe superficially attracted to one another. Be sure to have a strong foundation before getting too deep.

Fours and Sevens make for a dynamic, 'opposites attract' type of pairing, and the introvert coupled with an extrovert is a relatively common and successful partnership. Each half will need to be actively seeking to grow and learn from one another.

A Four matched with an Eight is sure to be a highly creative coupling. But with each partner having a penchant for being larger-than-life, beware of it quickly becoming more than you bargained for.

Nines and Fours can both be highly compassionate and empathetic, while also being quick and private. As long as there each half respects the other's privacy, this can be a very successful partnership.

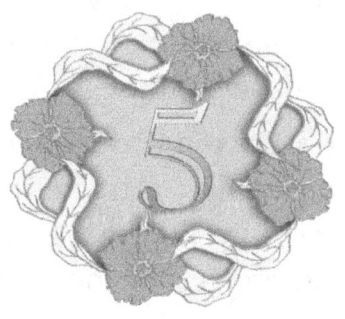

Type Five Relationships

A Five and a One tend to have a number of similarities; they are both intellectual and a little bit emotionally private. But while both types tend to be very fact-oriented, their individual ideas of what a fact is and how to arrive there can cause conflict.

Fives and Twos aren't the most common of pairings but when they do happen they tend to be highly complementary, given their opposite nature. While that can be fitting for some, it can lead to emotional imbalances where not all needs are always mutually met.

Another relatively opposite pairing, Fives and Threes are actually fairly common. Often it can be something of a creator-muse type of relationship, which can be highly rewarding, but also potentially dangerous, if one or both come to only be able to derive self-worth from the other.

Fives should be open to, but cautious of pairing up with Fours. Fours can certainly help Fives stay in touch with their emotions and feelings, but this type of relationship can become demanding for both.

Double Fives are an interesting combination. At least on the surface, another Five seems like a perfect fight for a Five, and that can be true, but beware that this relationship will be prone to overanalyzing and intellectualized over emotional.

Fives and Sixes both tend to have a primarily mental focus in life. This is often a type of relationship that starts as a friendship and becomes something more. Maintain open-mindedness for success.

Fives and Sevens both tend to have a lot of mental and intellectual energy. This can be positive and healthy for both. Be sure to address stress and conflict with care and patience.

Eights can be very complementary to a Five, and Fives can learn a lot of Eights. Power dynamics can play an ugly role if not careful though.

A Five paired with a Nine will be a good environment for emotional and personal space. A Five should seek out if a quiet, unobtrusive relationship is appealing; if not, fun away!

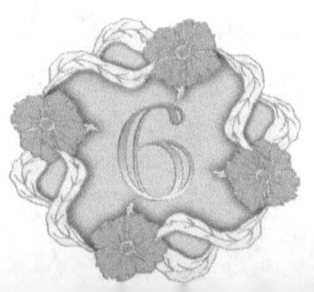

Type Six Relationships

Type Sixes should be aware that type Ones often misidentify as Sixes because they are so similar. This can lead to heavy judgment and criticism, so be aware.

Sixes and Twos tend to be very responsible and supportive toward each other. A control dynamic could quickly present itself though.

Threes don't pair very often with Sixes, but when it works, it really works. Be prepared to put in a lot of time and energy to keep it healthy and stable.

Fours tend to be drawn to Sixes, so they may well come to you. You'll likely feel like kindred spirits, but mutual fixations of abandonment issues can lead to emotional troubles.

Fives can bring some healthy critical thinking into a relationship with a Six, but you'll both have very different ways of thinking, so make sure to make communication and trust a priority.

A Six paired with another Six can make a strong couple. They tend to have a deep understanding of one another, which can make for a strong, trusting relationship. Don't let too much negativity enter the relationship though, as emotions will deteriorate quickly.

Another highly mental pairing, Sevens can bring a good deal of healthy stimulation to a Six. They can bring much joy and happiness into a relationship. However, a Six may perceive a Seven to be too unstable and unpredictable, so self-awareness and honesty are key.

A Six and Eight have the ability to create a very strong, healthy, long-term relationship. It will be highly supportive, deep and solid. However, both types can have a tendency to conceal emotions and weaknesses, so openness and complete trust are very important.

A very common and healthy relationship, Sixes and Nines tend to be stable and highly secure. Each type provides what the other needs. But there is such a thing as too much of a good thing, so be careful not to get too comfortable with the relationship or it could quickly become stagnant and cease to grow and develop.

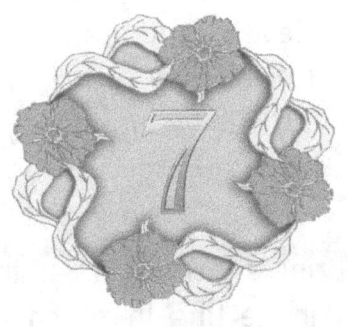

Type Seven Relationships

Ones can bring a lot of good habits and attention to detail into a relationship with a Seven, which can be very important in a Seven's life. But on the flip side, if there isn't strong teamwork and cooperation, the One may begin to perceive the Seven as being undisciplined and immature.

A Two paired with a Seven is a generally fun, outgoing and high-energy relationship. A Two will bring in some emotional depth that a Seven may lack, but the Seven may begin to feel suffocated and held back after a while.

Another high-quality pairing, a Three will be very compatible with a Seven in terms of energy levels and tendency to be outgoing. Three may bring a level of sensitivity to the relationship, but the constant high energy may lead to emotional burnout.

Four can bring a lot to a Seven in terms of focus and in getting in touch with their feelings. Fours and Sevens tend to have a high degree of early attraction, which could lead to immediate sparks, but strongly aligned interests and pursuits are important if that level of interest is to be maintained.

Sevens and Fives tend to make good reciprocal pairings. Fives can bring a degree of self-reliance and independence to a Seven, for whom those things may not be a priority, however, under stress, Fives may tend to detach emotionally, so the Seven must be aware of this.

Sixes can have a strong reinforcing effect in a relationship with a Seven. They tend to compliment a Seven's ability to think outside the box with concrete steps and plans. However, beware of developing conflicting goals.

A relationship formed from a double Seven pairing can be spotted from a mile away. Very high energy, fun and spontaneous, and always the entertainers. However, the potential trouble spots are just as easy to see; a relationship primarily characterized by wish-fulfillment and throwing caution to the wind can become unhealthily hedonistic in a hurry.

An Eight and Seven pairing tend to be very strong-willed and assertive. It can also be very practical and thoughtful, but if either partner doesn't have a healthy outlet for their energies, it could become a big problem.

Sevens paired with Nines are one of the more common pairings seen. They can both be very positive and optimistic, with Nines bringing a particularly calming, steadying nature to the relationship. This pairing is often very successful and good at defusing problems, just be careful to be aware of what your partner isn't

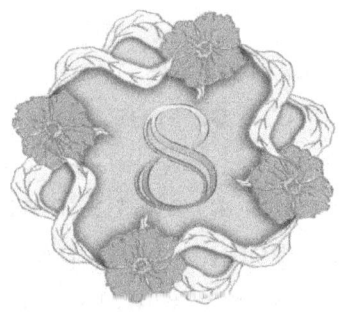

communicating.

Type Eight Relationships

One's can be highly attracted to Eights, so keep an eye out. They will bring will and energy into the relationship, but cracks can begin to show after a while because of the opposite nature of the two.

Twos have a lot in common with Eights. Expect a lot of passion and vitality in the relationship, but differences in interpersonal relationships could lead to problems.

Eights and Three can work together quite nicely, and Eights nature can be quite comforting and supportive for a Three, but both partners must know their limits in order to not become over-worked, and bring stress into the relationship.

Fours can be an excellent pair with an Eight if you're looking for a highly creative and stonily emotional connection. However, those emotional connections could become impassioned arguments if not careful.

Eights and Fives generally make for really good pairs, with Fives helping Eights to be more empathetic and thoughtful. However, insecurity could play a strong role here, so be aware.

Eights and Sixes tend to be a very strong and concrete pair. They tend to be quick to trust each other, but trust can backfire.

Eights and Sevens make for strong, trail-blazing partners. But a high-energy, productive pair could become a trap for misplaced anger if not careful.

The double Eight pair is one of energy and vitality. But it can also be highly volatile and ego can begin to play a role.

Meanwhile, Nines tend to look up to Eights, which can be powerful in the short-term, but lead to unhealthy power imbalance in the long-term.

Type Nine Relationships

Nines and Ones tend to be attracted to one another, but not always for the best. Each has very different ways of approaching problems, which can be a major issue if not handled correctly.

Nines and Twos are often very similar in a lot of ways, with both being nurturing in nature. Communications breakdown can become a problem early on if not established early.

A fairly common partnership, Threes tend to help Nines value themselves more fully. This generally is a positive and healthy thing, just be careful not to become complacent.

Fours have a tendency to bring out more expressiveness of feelings in Nines. That's definitely a positive, just make sure not to become disengaged or distant.

Fives often have the ability to draw an emotional connection out of Nines. But tensions can start to take hold early, so be prepared to address them, or let them go.

Nines and Sixes make for a very firm and stable relationship, with Sixes bringing a certain inquisitiveness and mental element to the table. However, both partners must be comfortable speaking their minds and addressing concerns or else problems will fester under the surface.

Nines paired with Sevens are very common, having a healthy combination of similar and complementary qualities. Sevens can bring a strong element of fun and a sense of adventure to the relationship. But while this can be a very happy and positive pair, be careful to not ignore the negative or pretend there are no issues, as that will only make them worse.

Eights and Nines both tend to have strong leadership qualities. This can make for a focused, purposeful pair, or it can lead to the issue of each partner vying for supremacy, so cooler heads must prevail for this pair to succeed.

And finally, a double Nine pairing is one of the more common double pairs, as a Nine is in fact quite well suited to support and encourage other Nines. This will be a very steady, stable pair, but that can be a double-edged sword, as anything, even external elements, that upsets that stability can be a major problem.

Chapter 9: The Three Amigos

You can easily understand how our instincts relate to the stages of growth and then

fulfill their purpose by manifesting in our personality types. For example, think

about writing a book. First, you need an idea. Then you get your idea on paper.

Next, you try your best to get published either in print or online. The simple

analogy that works. What you will notice is that there is a definitive moment of

shift as the book comes to fruition. However, the result is out of our control. The

completion of the process occurs once it is read!

We are born with innate abilities. We know how to breathe the moment we are

born. We involuntarily cry when we are disappointed. Our personalities are built the same way our physiological bodies are. We begin with something prearranged

and expand its affect. If you study the Enneagram outside of your current,

incredible choice of reading, you will discover that our Three Amigos are also

referred to as subtypes. The instincts are categorized as SELF-PRESERVATION, SOCIAL,

and INTIMATE. When they are separately combined with the nine personality types

you get 27 Instinctive Variations.

Our personalities are quite complex, but the Enneagram gives us a visual

explanation and simplifies the ages old question: "Who are we?" To make this more

interesting, we do get a say so in how we prioritize our instincts. Our values

determine how these amigos stack up. It can easily be illustrated by a stack of

donuts. Your favorite on the top, second favorite squished in the middle and your least favorite lying on the bottom. Our behaviors are directly related to which donut

is our favorite.

Maybe you value sex more than self-preservation or an adaptive nature. Voilà. You

will quickly notice that your personality traits develop around the nature of

relationships. How they evolve depends on how healthy you are as a person. Sex is

then characterized as your dominant instinct. Perhaps that is how Joe Eszterhas

came up with BASIC INSTINCT.

Self-preservationists prefer that their surroundings change to accommodate them.

They focus on physical needs and security. The absolutely beautiful thing about

this subtype is that they will also seek preservation for others. I think it is fair to

say that our world needs people who are naturally drawn to taking care of the security of others.

Our Social butterflies want what is best for all of us! They will adapt to their

environments if that best serves the situation. Additionally, you'll find them as

open, warm-hearted, and good at making connections with others. Socially

dominant people prefer long-term relationships and creating a difference in their

communities.

Now that we have gone over the instincts separately let us now talk about how they

can intermingle. Just when you might have thought all of this had some simplicity!

We humans never cease to amaze so it is important to know that you can exhibit

more than one instinctual variant. It is quite possible to possess two and avoid the

third.

We choose whether to embrace our instincts as an asset or steer clear of it as a liability. Unfortunately, if we fixate on that negativity and become consumed by

the fear behind it, we highlight our weakest link.

Chapter 10: The Benefits Of Really Knowing Who You Are

Perhaps you remember from the beginning of this book that I mentioned that five years ago I started turning my life around. I first had to discover who I was in order to truly be able to reshape who I wanted to be. When you apply for a job, often the prospective employer will give you personality tests. They want to measure how you would likely perform within their firm's environment. They want to make sure that they invest in the right person for the job, and by utilizing these types of tests, they have a good sense of whom you are and how you would behave in certain circumstances.

This is the same principle that occurs when you are on a journey of personal transformation. You will benefit from knowing more about yourself, including your personality type, and you will be able to adjust your actions in order to accomplish your goals. You will also learn that it can be helpful to know the personality types of the people with whom you interact on a regular basis.

Let's first review some of the benefits from examining your particular personality traits.

Professional life

Think about it for one minute — the more you know about yourself, the better career choices you can make. This is true early on in your life when the school counselor helps you take these types of tests to identify and evaluate your skills and your personality type so they can better advise you on what career path would best suit you. Unfortunately, life does not always allow us to go with the career that is the most fitted to our personality. For example, you may wish to be an artist or musician but you have to support yourself and others, so you perform a job that has nothing to do with art or music. However, often when we realize that we are unhappy with in our profession, we are able to come back to our roots later on, and figure out where we went astray.

I've always loved writing, and also always had a passion for languages. Although for a while I thought being a journalist was the obvious career choice for me, I am far too careful and solitary a person to be a journalist. I actually worked for many years in customer service because I have a very strong desire to help people. Yet I felt that there was always something missing in my professional life. I had to finally accept that as much as I wanted to help people, I am definitely a loner. I prefer to work alone and be my own boss. So being an entrepreneur seemed to be the optimal choice for me, right?

Maybe, but then that choice is risky for me too, because I fall under the peacemaker category. I highly dislike confrontation, and seek justice. In order to do so, I have a tendency to avoid relationships all together. My permanent career change happened a few years back, where I decided to work from home, even if it would mean a slightly lower salary than what I could earn in the corporate world.

As an independent interpreter and freelance writer, I can now say I am totally professionally satisfied. I can help many customers over the phone to get around their language barriers and also help them communicate better. I can also write many self-help books and assist many readers on diverse subjects.

I have accepted my natural inclination to want to work alone, and stopped fighting that personality trait of mine. However, I also recognized my strong need to help others, and wanted to combine both of those aspects of my personality with the perfect career choice for me. It took me over twenty years to figure it out, but it was all worth it. Everything I did before led me to where I am today. All I really had to do was to follow my natural traits and desires, and I ended up where I wanted to be, and where I needed to be professionally, all along.

There's no need to make sudden career changes that would put yourself or your family in a difficult financial situation. But if you realize now that you are unhappy about your current place of employment or field of work, I can guarantee you that it has something to do with your personality type. Don't ask someone who is a personality type "Achiever" to sit in a cubicle taking orders all day. So in summary, discovering your personality type will help you tremendously in choosing the right career path for you. You will probably experience require some trials and errors along the way, but once you discover what career path best for you, you will be relieved and happy. After all, you probably spend an average of 8 hours a day, or 40 hours a week or more working, so it makes a lot of sense to thrive to be the best and the happiest that you can be at what you do. Life is way too short to be miserable at work.

Your Social life

The key to improving your social life lies not only in the fact that you will know and embrace who you actually are, but you will also gain a better understanding of other people as well. If you get a good handle on the different types of personalities that exist, you will accept that people can think and act very differently from the way that you think. This does not mean that there is something wrong with you or them, just that you are each different. This knowledge will free you from being overly judgmental and may give you a better chance to get to know someone new. You can learn to accept that their personality type makes them think or act a certain way that is perhaps the opposite of how you would act in the same situation.

Your Personal Relationships

Your relationships can be greatly impacted not only by the personality under which you identify, but also in your ability to understand someone else's personality type. This especially applies in a relationship of a couple. It's important to understand the difference between partners, because there will always be some variances. Even if you have discovered that you have the same personality type as your partner, there will always be aspects that are slightly different. For example, you might be a loyalist, but also have very strong enthusiast traits as well.

Solving conflicts will be much easier once you learn more about yourself. You can better predict when you are getting angry, sad, or even predict exactly how you would react in a certain situation. You can avoid embarrassing yourself in certain situations, or train yourself to react better, or more positively. Also, knowing how your loved ones will react depending on their personality type will promote respect and understanding instead of bickering and fighting.

When I started becoming more comfortable with whom I truly was, I started being happier. Accepting my personality and molding my life in consequence, and ending my fight with whom I truly was, liberated me. There will always be people who don't agree with what you do and how you do it, and I was always so afraid to do anything that seemed out of place. I was terrified to take risks or make any changes. Don't get me wrong, I still like my security, and would not wildly invest my retirement funds in a risky stock market account.On the other hand, I don't have a problem being a freelance writer and dealing with the unexpected aspects of this part-time job.

Your Children

If you are a parent, the chance to understand your children better is another great reason for taking the time to find what your personality type is as well as discovering your child's personality type. You can certainly guide your child better if you have a basic understanding of their natural characteristics and how they might react to certain situations. You can learn to adjust your reactions, the consequences to their bad behavior or, even the way you talk to them or reward them.

My journey allowed me to understand that as a peacemaker, I was prone to fighting other people's injustices for them. This is not a bad thing in and of itself, but it is not necessarily the healthiest thing for others, who may need to learn from their own mistakes. For example, for many years, I interfered between my son and other people, just because I was trying to protect him from getting hurt.Eventually, a few years ago, I realized that my son needed to start fighting his own battles, and that overprotecting him was not doing him any favors. Although many people had told me before was about the errors of my ways, and how I was over-controlling, I never wanted to hear it. However, when I faced my personality type and accepted that I was indeed interfering far too much in my son's life, I learned to step back, and this behavior did better my relationship with him.

Chapter 11: Important Folks And Written Records

Here we go then with a bit of information about the important folks of the Enneagram.

All the way back in AD 375 a Greek Philosopher called **Evagrius** proposed 'the 8 evil thoughts' which it is generally accepted was the seed of the Enneagram. Also it was used by Pope Gregory the Great as the basis of his seven deadly sins.

George Gurdieff (1870) founded a school of thought known as the Fourth Way. Gurdieff was an Armenian mystic having learnt from a secret Middle Eastern School immersed in teachings from two thousand years' hence. There was no personality typing at this point.

Teaching centred around the idea that there are three brains which dominate human behaviour. These three brains are centred in the Gut, the Heart and the

Intellect. These form the three Triads of the Enneagram.

This is where we begin. You will see that the 'Triads' form the first part of your Typing Tunnel.

Do you think of yourself as an instinctual person, often acting out of instinct and then maybe regretting it later? We all operate from all three aspects of the Triads, though one is usually paramount. I warn you now, that it is notoriously difficult to type yourself and it is usually by reflection and pondering on the ideas and opinions others have to you that the typing begins. However, it is so very easy to type other people!

Enneagram and the Kabbalah

Anyone who has learned anything about the workings of the mind, particularly counseling, mentalism or hypnotherapy, recognises that often the patterns in our lives seem to escape reason.

Our dilemma often is 'tell me... why on earth do I continue to do this thing that I consciously do not want to do anymore?!'

We open up the whole debate of 'determinism' and 'chaotic free will' : do you choose to believe that your life is predetermined and written in the stars for you to act out or do you believe that your life is created moment by moment by each decision, action and thought you conjure?

Can we solve this argument by suspending our judgements and considering that both approaches could possibly be true?

The Tree of Life from the mystical tradition of the Kabbalah and this Enneagram from further back into Greek philosophy we can dare to tread, offer some insights and explanations.

From here we speak in terms of energies, not behaviour.

It saddens me that folks so quickly rush to the internet and 'type' themselves, satisfied, or dissatisfied with their findings and then discard the rest of the information in smugness or defiance!

You see, the same energy can be interpreted in different ways and this is where we are truly magical, individual Beings.

For example, a typical type 9 person sitting quietly at the dinner party may be interpreted as shy by one personality type and rude by another. Trust me. I'm a 9!

'Ah, someone go talk to Jennie, she's all on her own', or 'Well, if she doesn't want to be bothered joining in, then leave her be, you think she'd make the effort, how rude!'

The 9 might be just contemplating the deliciousness of the dessert, or silently pleading the 8 to shut up and leave them alone, who knows!

A 7 might find adventure and pleasure saturation in a bowl of custard, a forbidden drug, or challenging themselves to conquer the peak of the next mountain, who knows!

Whilst the Kabbalah depicts and explains energies and their polarities at a micro and macro level, the Enneagram focusses on how those energies are expressed from a personality viewpoint. The destructive energy of Geburah, for example, can work its way into expression in the 9 as a shutting down, a retreating, whilst the 8 can utilise it to feel more alive and thrive upon stripping down old outworn systems and implementing the new dynamism of change.

Ultimately, the Kabbalah teaches at its fundamental level that only two things exist. 1) the Creator and 2) the Creature.

The Creature (us) is focused upon receiving pleasure and does so in a variety of ways. It also seeks to avoid pain – at all costs. The fall from Grace happened when the Creature sought to be like the Creator.

In striving so hard to be Creator-like the Creature forgot/denied the Creator existed and thus began an emptiness, a profound loneliness – a separation from all else.

In our attempts to heal the wound of this separation, which began with the biggest wound of all, in childhood, we developed our personalities.

Of course, you can spot differing personalities in little children quite early on, though the negative part of the personality, the contriving, the manipulating, the power playing parts of us, grew over time, so that we could co-exist in an envious and competitive world.

We fell. We fell into one of 9 categories, or types of personality.

Chapter 12: The Helper

Synopsis

You can simply rely on them to give some assistance. These individuals live to serve and they appreciate doing it simultaneously!

This part discusses:

- What an aide is about
- Why are aide great to have around
- What is most troublesome about aides
- Dealing with them and drawing out the best
- Who they coexist with
- Who they don't alongside

Living in administration and commitment to others is the center structure of an aide – figure out how to acknowledge them, comprehend them for who they are and bring the best out of them!

What Is A Helper?

Aides live to serve. The length of they feel that they are in commitment to others, they feel they are commendable. A being of benevolence, they accept that providing for others is their most noteworthy calling as they feel that affection is the most vital feeling on the planet.

These are the hottest, most accommodating individuals around who will always remember your birthday (or feel truly regretful when they do as such...) and will go the additional mile to help one in need.

An outgoing individual in nature, they endeavor to relate and show adoration to all their loved ones. They live for gratefulness and frequently falls into the trap of keeping an eye on the needs of others at the disregard they could call their own which regularly causes an issue.

The Good

Partners love the unbounded feeling of flexibility which incorporates opportunity of expressive their adoration to the world. An expressive being on unequivocal affection, they long to give and give and give until they can give no more.

Assistants are profoundly unselfish – you can simply rely on them to yield themselves for the benefit of other people, regularly at their own cost.

Being around them is great on the grounds that they will dependably be there to satisfy your needs and feel their love.

The Bad

The issue with aides is that they have a solid propensity to look for vainglory in view of their affection to help other people. Since they feel that being in commitment to others is their most prominent calling, they will do whatever it takes, even to the point of control with a specific end goal to get individuals to recognize their accommodation. They are inclined to bootlicking.

A few aides, unexpectedly… despite the fact that they are loaded with affection, can turn truly monstrous if their adoration is not responded. They feel that they are saints in light of the adoring and helping nature, they will continually have a feeling of qualification to those nearest to them – frequently feeling that individuals owe them thankfulness and appreciation.

At the point when their enthusiastic needs go unmet, they come truly bossy and manipulative in light of the fact that they have earned their a good fit for response. At the very least case situation, they may get to be crazy, nonsensical, extremely hard to manage and even oppressive!

Instructions to Deal With Them

The best thing an aide can accomplish for themselves is to deal with their own needs actually when they feel full on in helping other people. The length of they are kept from burnout, they are less defenseless to passionate depletion and dryness. They regularly expect that they are unworthy for others to adore them.

A self protecting assistant will help other people and frequently decline to enlighten others regarding their own needs. To help these individuals, you need to help them back behind the foundation else they will feel that you are interrupting their self-esteem without understand that they are running on an unfilled fuel tank.

A sexual assistant will need heaps of adoration and consideration communicated noticeably or outwardly. They must be recognized by their mates or they will breakdown. Be quiet when listening to their wandering requirements for affirmation and help them to help themselves and you'll do fine.

Social assistants are great in magnanimous associations or guiding focuses. Issuing them great social tasks is alright the length of the individuals they are serving give loads of consolation and backing. Deal with their needs when you see that they are serving an excess of individuals or they understand smoldered with the tremendous weight or attempting to please everybody.

They work exceptionally well with individualists (sort 7) who are regularly profoundly complex and have a wide range of requirements (which assistants affection to be around and help them) and they loathe being around challengers (sort 8) who undermine their safe places.

Chapter 13: Type Four: The Unique Caregiver

In This Chapter:

Living a life of passion

Everyday living versus living on the edge
Including pain as part of the mix

The agony and the ecstasy Be authentic or die

Identifying the Four in Yourself and Others

If you have a Four in the family, you know it! Four's moods tend to go up and down from depression to elation, from brooding to thrill seeking. When Four exaggerates out of playfulness they can easily be mistaken for another type, such as Seven. At other times Fours can exaggerate feelings as a way of testing for emotional reality.

Nonverbal cues

If the eyes are truly the mirror of the soul, look deeply into the eyes of the Four and you will see depth. They may have beautiful, fluid hand movements, or a graceful or unique walking style. Four's individuality shows up in unique self-expressed ways of dressing. Fours dress for mood and often change clothes as moods change.

Clues to spotting the Four are:

Intense mood swings, from joy to despair

A history of dramatic intense relationships, short or long-lasting, Passionate expressions

Push-pull in relationships A tendency to cry

verbal cues

A Four talks at length about relationships, feelings, their need for engagement with others, whether others are rejecting them, what is lacking in others, what is missing in themselves, what they long for and what they dream about. They use words and themes that inspire intense feeling in others. They love to talk about the extremes of life and death, abandonment and reconnection, agony and ecstasy. They are delighted when they are understood but can also magnify slight misunderstandings.

Other verbal cues include: Dramatic, emphatic words

Focusing on pain or what could go wrong
Seductive, romantic language

Storytelling with rich, emotional detail

Emotional vocabulary with dramatic undertones, hints, nuances

Fours in caregiving

Unique Fours feel the turmoil of these times with a special poignancy. Whether female or male, they long to be seen and valued for who they are—intriguing, gifted, and unlike anyone else. While others want to be appreciated and loved, Fours yearn for it. They look for meaning in every moment, milking life experience for beauty and emotional truth. If you're a Four, there's plenty in caregiving to feed your needs, but what about your Loved

One? Beware of adding unnecessary drama to your Loved One's life.

As a Four, you slide naturally into meaningful service. You measure life by special moments (so plentiful at this time of life) that transcend the mundane, where life soars to special heights or plummets to deep despair. This emotional roller coaster gives you the depth of experience that makes life worth living. Others may think you're too focused on yourself or are just enjoying yourself too much.

Your talent for immersion in emotion can be a gift to some others, teaching them to feel deeply at this time, helping them to remember that we come from spirit, and reminding them to live with and express their full range of emotions. Exploration of feelings and soul-searching are more central and accessible nowadays, but beware of unrealistic expectations of others—some just won't be able to go easily to a place of strong emotions, or perhaps at all. Some may even find your emotional honesty to be more than they can handle.

Four's Positive Traits

All types have room for improvement, and to the Four, that is good news. Fours tackle personal growth the way they tackle life, with passion for a challenge.

Feeling a Range of Emotions - You are the only type committed to feeling every aspect of life, never shying away from pain, loss, or joy. If it is real and true, you want to feel it. Suffering is part of life as much as the positive and you don't want to miss a moment, so this time as a nurturer is fertile ground.

Courage - You have the courage to show what you feel, for the sake of beauty and the emotional truth of experience. You take on seemingly

impossible projects that to others may seem hopeless. You don't mind being the one who exposes what is real and can be a role model for others in expressing their individuality. You take great joy in transforming the pain of others, making it worthwhile. In many ways, you are a hero.

Empathy - Because of your love of intimacy, communication with your Loved One can reach new levels at this time, depending on her/his type. For you, the tone, nuance, and emphasis of language is as important as what is said, so you will be more tuned in than most to the feelings of your Loved One. You inspire authentic emotional expression in yourself and others.

Four's Challenges

Our culture is hard on Fours. If you are a male Four, your emotions of sadness, grief, or fear, are perceived, even now, as feminine. We are raised with a sexist bias for rationality and stoicism versus high emotionality. This is one of your crosses to bear, but you don't let it stop you.

Monkey-mind - Your intensified thoughts and feelings create an ever-changing "reality" that swings from ecstasy to despair. You are the lead actor on the stage of high drama, a marionette with your feelings pulling your strings.

Ungrounded Drama - You shy away from stability, mistaking it for boredom, yet you long for security, ease, and acceptance even as you generate emotional turmoil. These times bring enough drama for everyone without you generating more.

Self-reference - Your longing for what you don't have takes up so much space in your heart that there is little room for real happiness. Your focus on your own feelings may make you inaccessible to others. When you don't get the attention you want, resentment further distances others.

Four's Opportunities for Personal Growth

You tend to intensify life, which makes you alive, but are you limiting yourself by not having a more neutral approach? Enjoy life and see life from acceptance and your value, rather than from rejection and abandonment. Focus on what is good. For Fours to grow, take these steps

Mind Your Thoughts - You create much of your unwanted reality, but your prodigious creativity is your ally in gaining control. Think of yourself as a magician and reinvent your emotional experience by playing with your thoughts. Choose new ones and watch your mood shift. For instance, as you visit the sometimes depressing nursing home yet again, imagine that you are a heroic missionary sent to bring comfort and that someday an inspiring movie will be made about you. You are the source of your feelings. When you find yourself competing for special attention, focus on trusting that the love you seek will come naturally.

Practice Centering - Centering practices such as breathing techniques, visualization, and meditation bring clarity, countering your tendency to be ungrounded or scattered. Managing your inner life in a more grounded way can have a profound effect on your Loved One— others react to our energy, resisting or compounding whatever we are creating. Humor is also and always a useful antidote for the prevalent dramas.

It's Not All About You - Growth for the Four comes in realizing that not everything has deep meaning or is personal. Rather than focusing on what you don't have, focus on self-love, with gratitude for what you do have. Self-love will heal the pain of longing as you diminish your neediness, freeing you up for real connection and relationship with your Loved One.

Stay neutral and be objective - For you, it is terribly hard at times not go to extremes. When you are hurting, your surges of thoughts and feelings may be telling you that everything is falling apart or that the end is near. But hold steady. Things may not be as bad as they seem. Remember, you are not alone—everyone experiences the fear of loss. Don't catastrophize. Just because you think it, doesn't mean it is true. Stay calm by focusing on your breathing, get some objective feedback, and take care of yourself. Be in your body and slow down.

Focus on the positive - The good often attracts more good. That may sound superficial, but it is helpful. Think and write about what is working. The things that are good can come from a seemingly bad situation. Don't make it worse by focusing on what isn't working.

Don't exaggerate - Looking through your lens, you are not exaggerating. You are feeling what you feel and it is intense. Highs and

lows swing back and forth. Doubt your feelings at times - they may be more intense than what is happening in reality. If you are starting to amplify your feelings or personal story, catch yourself. Don't seek out extra attention by making your feelings much bigger than they are.

Love yourself - You want to be loved by special others, but yearning won't help you or your relationships. Shift your focus to loving yourself, valuing your emotions, your love of creativity and aesthetics. Lessen your demand that others love you. Nobody can take care of all the pain or loss now or from your childhood. Don't load that onto anyone, especially your Loved One. Make a list of all your valuable qualities; all that is working and what you can provide to yourself. See yourself as special and unique, without needing others to do that for you.

Listen to others - You do listen and are often highly empathic, particularly if someone has an intense decision or dilemma, but you sometimes become bored by those whose lives are mundane. Listen to others as much as you want to be listened to, and you will have the adoration you seek. Be careful to not repeat your story endlessly or demand unequal attention, or your friends may tire. Check in with them, on occasion, to catch this tendency.

Create to Recreate - Draw, paint, sculpt, sing, dance, or write. You were meant to create and need avenues for expressing your inner self and desires in the world. Especially now, if you deny that need you may implode and lose yourself in your intensity. Spend at least some time with creative pursuits and you will benefit, as will your Loved One and others who gain from your personal experience joy.

Spend some time with other Fours - Only Fours can really understand the world of a Four, and will appreciate your intensity and depth. Give yourself the release of sharing your art, crying your eyes out, talking about life and death, and going as deep as you want.

Four's Heart, soul, and Mind

In practice, a Four's heart and soul drive her mind. If you are a Four, flip that around, manage life more with your mind, and watch your caregiving become less turbulent and your life more grounded in spirit.

Fours in Relationships

Fours are empathic, particularly if their Loved One is taking a risk, struggling with a major decision, or is simply being honest or vulnerable. Four's ability to embrace the pain of others is a source of comfort to many receiving a Four's caring, but families vary in the degree to which they can support the Four's own expression of feelings.

As a Four, you seek authenticity from others and attempt to live your own life authentically. Fours feel so deeply and love that depth. You may feel that relationships now are even more emotionally complex and more of a struggle, but that is not necessarily a bad thing. Attachment to a Loved One can be strong and a loving care-partnering relationship can be ecstatic. But while struggle lets you know you're alive, too much can tip the Four over into abandonment, and to a Four, abandonment is death. If the Loved One is a parent, the idea of them dying can be torturous.

For some family members, who may want to learn how to create a deeper experience with their Loved One, Four's capacity for depth and authenticity may be especially valued now. However for some others, Four's self-focus can be trying. As the tensions of caregiving heighten their critical or judgmental side, they may find fault with your feeling-based style, describing you as dramatic, intense, exaggerated, or indulgent. The possibility of being judged and rejected is one of your hardest burdens.

Joy, ecstasy, rapture and positive feelings are also welcome to Fours, but nothing in the boring middle is of interest. To the Four, the day- to-day sameness of life in a nursing home, with its mundane chats and pleasantries, may seem worse than dying. With an addiction to drama, the Four can bring trouble into the nursing home, trailing after her like ill-mannered children, upsetting the peaceful climate that others have worked hard to create.

Relationship Advice - If life at times seems boring, be careful of the dramas you create. You and those around you can't afford excessive emotional indulgence right now. Focus more on the needs of others, and when you find your thoughts taking you on a downward spiral, turn them around. Learn skills for navigating deep emotions from the left-brained members of your family or support team. Developing strong boundaries will let you be empathetic to others' experience without losing yourself. And when others can't fully reciprocate, manage your own emotions by daily journaling, or talking to a participative and no-nonsense therapist.

Four's spiritual side

For the Four, deep meaning makes life worth living. You want enlightened experiences, special moments of beauty. You are always searching for mystery, the unseen, the seed buried in the ground with potential for life. You sense that caregiving can be fertile ground for mining such deep meaning, but not everyone wants to go there.

You are fascinated by death and what happens after death, so you easily engage in the larger questions that arise when thinking about a Loved One nearing the end of life. You may believe in past lives and that reality doesn't stop when the body dies, making it more possible to contemplate your Loved One's end. You are always exploring what is unspoken, seeking your version of God to transform everyday life into one that has more meaning. You may be drawn to esoteric forms of religion, listen to your inner spirit, consult intuitives, or use tarot cards and crystals.

A Spiritual Lesson - Find those who can love joining you in exploration of the unknown, but if others don't want to go, let them be. Accept their differences and don't take it personally.

As a Four, you may teach others to be open to the extraordinary, yet you need to see that the ordinary may have special moments as well. Yes, it is possible for you to go too deep while missing the life that is happening around you. Be careful not to self-reflect and process so much that you live solely from your insights and feelings at the expense of opportunities to take healthy risks and creative actions.

How Fours Think & Make Decisions

Fours think about ideals—ideal relationships, ideal meaning in life, ideal virtues. If you are a Four, you think about how to better understand your family, and how you aren't understood. You feel and analyze what is going on in your relationships and how they could be better. You focus on what needs to be changed in you, what is wrong with you, and how you could have a richer experience. You also think about your enjoyments— rich sensual textures and colors, subtle fragrances, and visual delights.

Four's inner conversations are:

I don't feel understood. If only (s)he would listen to me. I feel so rejected by that comment.

This is deep for me. No one gets it. I'm bored out of my mind.

There is too much crisis in my life.

Your decisions often arise from this self-preoccupation, since they are born of your perceived or imagined needs. You may then turn to worst- case scenarios to guide your actions, or take a crisis orientation, rather than proceeding in a measured, more balanced, or realistic way.

Four's Thought/Action Alternatives

Constantly measuring yourself and life against some ideal creates the preconditions for suffering. How you think really does create your reality, so wield those powerful thoughts carefully. You might just as easily generate the thought that you are loved, valued, and valuable. Remember, you are the thought wizard. Your happiness does not rely on figuring out others or external circumstances. Enjoy the game of understanding life, yourself, and others, but watch for that moment when your thoughts begin to undermine your well-being.

What Four would like to be able to say: (S)he understands me well enough.

Most of her comments are positive. This is only a feeling. My Four friend will get it even if others don't.

So I'm bored. Not the end of the world. What can I create now? I feel less crisis-oriented knowing that others have problems like mine.

Decisions are important and have consequences. Those that arise from balanced and forgiving thoughts will make your days more deeply satisfying. At the very least, when your feelings are overwhelming and you believe you must make a decision, it may be best to wait or at least get feedback from a friend. Think before acting! Broaden your perspective first to take the big picture into account.

Making the Most of Being a Four

The Four's type modifiers, Stress Type, Growth Type, and Wings, nuance her experience, offering many more options for how to feel. Optional ways of being allow the Four to fine tune her skills at being happy.

Four's stress Type - The Heartfelt Two

Growth Type - The Precise one

When under stress, Fours usually move toward Type Two, the Helper/Cheerleader. As tensions build, Fours see giving as a way to feel better. If they are less well-developed and their abandonment fears have kicked in, their giving will come from the worst traits of their Helper Stress Type—they will give out of neediness while seeking attention for their giving, expecting appreciation in return. Giving from deprivation can backfire when your Loved One responds by feeling manipulated or disempowered.

A more mature Four will be able to respond to stress by giving from generosity, from a genuine place of caring, abundance, and appreciation, the best traits of Two. When you do this, you'll feel happy and balanced, focusing less on what you are not getting and more on what is working. Focusing on the positive increases the positive and is always a good remedy for you if you're a Four.

To achieve a place of even greater strength, Fours can also choose to

move to their Growth Type, Type One, The Precise Caregiver, which allows the Four to go beyond personal truth to focus on the objective truth of ethics and right action. Now the Four can fall back on accepted time-honored principles and guidelines for living. By adding this higher side of One, Fours can see that they aren't alone. Everyone struggles. You can join others to live, not only the tragic and the comic, but also the joy of everyday events.

Four's Wings - The Achieving Three &The Knowledgeable Five

Four's wings, The Achieving Caregiver Three and Knowledgeable Five, offer unique twists on the Four story. The Three wing benefits the Four by bringing her out of herself to focus on success. Western culture encourages this shift—business people are more rewarded than artists, and so these Fours are often mistyped as Threes. Three qualities help to moderate the Four caregiver, making her less self-focused and more action-focused. The Four/Three can take the lead as the Loved One's advocate while still creating connection and special moments.

The Four with a strong Knowledgeable Five wing is more analytical and introverted than the Four/Three. The Four/Five struggles with success, living a more inner life. Their love of learning will keep them on top of the latest medical information, but their loner qualities can make this support role challenging if their Loved One is a type that craves high engagement. Since Fours and Fives are both individualistic, the Four/ Five is even more non-conformist than the Four/Three. She longs to be discovered for special qualities, and may live in a fantasy world, not the best place for handling the business aspects of caregiving. This is no fantasy, though with focus, the Four/Five's ability to bridge the worlds between feeling and thinking can be a great strength.

Four's Degrees of Balance

Well-balanced Fours have passion, depth, empathy, creativity, and an appreciation for differences, while being able to support others' growth and uniqueness.

You have an amazing aliveness, with no fear of exploring the dark side of life. You don't over-dramatize, yet you spice up life and

are perfect entertainers, making fun of life's quirks and complexities, while maintaining your center. This combination of lightness and depth is a powerful gift. You see the irony of your own life drama, the suffering, and even the humor within it, in a way that no other type does. If you can pass that on to your Loved One, you make his/her life all the easier. You don't use others to satisfy your needs. You are a natural giver. Your heart is open, and you are deeply compassionate. Sounds like the ideal caregiver!

Average Fours struggle between feeling the heights of emotion and daily pain, and being pulled toward boredom. The tendency for crisis orientation can exhaust the Four, not to mention their Loved One and family. Four's need for understanding adds another complication, as it can call for more than others are able to give at this time. Depression is a real danger.

Out-of-balance Fours are all story and self-pity, wanting to pull others on stage to act out various parts of anger, sadness, and irresponsibility. Solace may be sought in addiction. This is the victim, too preoccupied to give true caring. Easily damaging relationships, they will be blamed for causing others' pain. If this is you, notice how you are creating your own unhappiness and write a better script. Model yourself after others who can help you out of the mire. Until you are better able to balance yourself, let others do more of the hands-on work.

Chapter 14: Type Two Personality

Next in the list is the Type two personality. Individuals in this category are often referred to as the helper or giver.

The characteristics of Type Twos are as follows -

- Type Twos long for love and crave the feeling to be "needed" by others. They are often considered popular in any social group or environment such as a new school, church or neighborhood. These helpers/givers are also missed the most by their social peers when they leave.

In short, Type Twos can be described as a people person.

- They possess excellent human relations skills and get along with just about any kind of personality. Type two's try their best to avoid hostile situations with others. They are not confronting or aggressive. Type two's can adapt their speech and conduct to suit the individual they are relating with effortlessly. Type two's have incredible interpersonal abilities that may cause other people to ignore the shortcomings or weaknesses of a Type Two individual.

- Sometimes, Type Twos do not mind pleasing others and displeasing themselves. They are preoccupied with what others feel or think about them. Even when such opinions do not conform to reality, they make adjustments just to please that person.

- Type Twos are typically emotional and their relationship with the world revolves through their feelings for others. They often experience life and the world around them through their feelings. They possess a deep sense of empathy and find it easy to put themselves in the shoes of other people. When others turn a blind eye to the plight of an individual who is suffering, they are likely to come to the aid of that person.

- Type Twos can be nosey. They have a tendency to be very inquisitive about what is transpiring in the lives of others. They are often meddlesome and can sometimes keep sensitive people away from them but that would not stop them from trying to get close to such people. This directly results from an obsession to be over-caring and loving at all times, not minding whether the other person needs their attention at that moment or not.

- Sometimes, Type Twos may use their helping and giving nature to manipulate others and get them to do their bidding. They can pretend by showering love onto another person without the person's knowledge of such manipulations. On the flip side, others can easily use them because of their loyalty and love. They readily blend into different kinds of social groups or even different subgroups within a larger group.

- Type Twos can be too friendly to a fault and may not even notice when others have ill feelings towards them. This often ensures that they become likable even to the most difficult person to relate with. When they are hurt by others, they forgive quickly and are the first to make moves for reconciliation. This implies that they are quick to leave the past behind and get on with their lives.

- Type Two personalities are not just people persons, they are also people pleasers.

Type two's are usually optimistic in their approach to whatever they do. When others are seeing things from a negative perspective, they may help to change that perspective. They have a great amount of energy and they would rather 'see the donut and ignore the hole'. When they work with others in a team, they prioritize interaction with team members ahead of collective goals or rules.

Below is a list of renowned 'Type Two' personalities in human history -

JIMMY CARTER - an American politician who served his country as a senator, governor and finally as the 39th president. In 2002, he was awarded the Nobel Peace Prize for his work in co-founded the Carter Centre. The traits of a helper or giver in him were evident even after he left office as president. In 1982, he established the Carter Center to promote and expand human rights. He traveled extensively to conduct peace negotiations, monitor elections and advance disease prevention and eradication in developing nations.

MOTHER TERESA OF CALCUTTA - an Albanian-Indian Roman Catholic nun and missionary who was admired by the world over for her charity work that spanned over 130 countries. She was awarded the Nobel Peace Prize in 1979 and canonized by the Roman Catholic Church as a saint in 2016. Mother Teresa is a natural born helper. She devoted her whole life helping the poor and needy. She established the Missionaries of Charity, a Roman Catholic religious congregation which has over 4,500 sisters and manages homes for people living with HIV/AIDS, leprosy and tuberculosis. These homes also provided soup kitchens, dispensaries, mobile clinics, orphanages, and schools.

PRINCESS DIANA OF WALES - a member of the British royal family and first wife of the heir apparent to the British throne. She undertook royal duties on behalf of the Queen of England and represented her at functions overseas. She also received a lot of media attention for her charity work both locally and internationally. As a Type Two personality, she supported the International Campaign to Ban Landmines and was involved with dozens of charities including Great Ormond Street Hospital for children.

CELINE DION - A Canadian singer who has transformed from being a teen sensation to one of pop's music most influential voices. She has received five Grammy Awards and remains the best selling Canadian artist and also one of the best-selling artists of all time with record sales of over 250 million copies worldwide. The helping and giving personality enabled her to make giant strides in philanthropy. She has actively supported many charity organisations all over the world. She joined a number of celebrities, athletes and politicians in 2003 to support the World Children's Day, a global fundraising programme. Dion also offered financial assistance to the victims of Hurricane Katrina (2005) and held a fundraising event for the victims of the 2004 Asian Tsunami.

HARRY BELAFONTE - An American singer, songwriter, and actor who is reputed to be the King of Calypso for popularising the Caribbean musical style with an international audience in the 1950s. He has received numerous awards including the Grammy Lifetime Achievement Award, Emmy Award, National Medal of Arts and an Honorary Doctorate Degree in music. Being a classic Type Two, he has been an advocate for political and humanitarian causes such as the Anti-Apartheid Movement in the USA for Africa. Since 1987, he has been a UNICEF Goodwill Ambassador.

DESMOND TUTU - A South African Anglican cleric and theologian known for his work as an anti-apartheid and human rights activist. He was the first indigenous black African to occupy the offices of both the Bishop of Johannesburg and the Archbishop of Cape Town. He has received numerous awards including the Nobel Peace Prize and has published many books containing his sermons and speeches. He earned global respect for his uncompromising stand for justice and reconciliation and for his efforts during and after apartheid to strengthen his country.

JOHN TRAVOLTA - An American actor, film producer, dancer and singer who has starred in a number of movies over a period of four decades. He has received the Golden Globe Award for Best Actor in a Motion Picture and many other nominations and awards in his career. After his son's death in 2009, he established the Jett Travolta Foundation in his memory. As a non-profit organization, its mission was to help children with special needs. The foundation has also contributed to other non-profit organizations like the Oprah Winfrey

Leadership Academy and The Institutes for the Achievement of Human Potential.

FLORENCE NIGHTINGALE - An English social reformer and statistician who is widely regarded as the founder of modern nursing. She established the first secular nursing school which is now part of King's College in London. In recognition of her pioneering work in nursing, the Nightingale Pledge taken by new nurses and the Florence Nightingale Medal, the highest international distinction a nurse can achieve, were named in her honour. The International Nurses Day is celebrated around the world on her birthday. Having a natural tendency to help people, Nightingale organized to care for wounded soldiers in the Crimean War. She also trained other nurses to do the same and that was how nursing started as a profession. She was also passionate about social reforms including improving healthcare for all sections of British society, advocating better hunger relief in India, helping to abolish prostitution laws and expanding the acceptable forms of female participation in the workforce.

The typical roles played by Type Two's include -

• THE QUEEN BEE - Type Twos like to become the center of attraction in any group where they belong. They want to serve and be served by everyone in the group. More like a mother hen role, they are comfortable when attending to the needs of as many members as possible within the group.

• THE AGONY AUNT - They want to be the person everyone else goes to for advice concerning various life issues. This makes them good listeners and counselors or at least possess a tendency to become such. Type Twos are never tired of listening to the pains and plight of other people and are willing to offer a helping hand if they can.

• THE WELL-MEANING GOSSIP - Type Twos like to be the first to spread news around, whether good or bad. They want people to hear it first from them and in that way consider them as a reliable news source. They may not necessarily use gossip to wreck relationships but sometimes their small talk may have unintended consequences.

- THE GATEKEEPER - They want to function as an intermediary between the group and other groups or the outside world in general. So they want to be the first to be hinted on whatever information is going out or coming in into the group. Nothing transpires within the group without their knowledge of it.

- THE GUARDIAN ANGEL - They want people to acknowledge them as their guardian angel who has done them some good in the past. This way they hope to keep such people close and reliant on them for various kinds of needs. People like to run to them in times of trouble.

- THE JEWISH MOTHER - Type Twos have a tendency to be overprotective almost to a point of being a burden to those they are supposedly caring for. She is also a pillar of strength behind those that she cares for except that such care may sometimes be taken to an extreme.

- THE MATCHMAKER - They like to be seen as the person who introduced A to B or the liaison between conflicting parties. And they are quick to remind both parties of the vital role they played in bringing them together and establishing or maintaining the relationship between them.

- THE SELF-SACRIFICING CARER - Type Twos are not afraid to make sacrifices in their attempt to show care and love to others. They would readily demonstrate a sacrificial attitude even when the other person does not really deserve it.

- THE OLD GRANDMOTHER - They may prioritize the needs of others above their own all in an attempt to keep others happy and satisfied. They find their happiness in making others happy and meeting their needs. All they want is love and attention in return and may get frustrated if they don't get it.

- **THE SELF-APPOINTED MARTYR** - They consider themselves as the scapegoat within the group and are willing to suffer for crimes they have nothing to do with. They slip into this role willingly and would not mind staying there for as long as possible. They would readily speak out for the voiceless or oppressed members of the group.

Type Twos have an exceptional ability to decipher and interpret the emotions of others and also unravel their unconfessed needs and aspirations. They do this, sometimes unconsciously, to be able to meet those needs. Their identities are centered around what they can or have done for people around them and have no issues with boasting about such. Their positive side can be described using adjectives like adaptable, generous, empathic, caring, insightful and enthusiastic. Their negative side can be described using adjectives like possessive, hysterical, manipulative and overly accommodating.

The following careers would suit a Type Two personality - counseling, ministry work (religion), teaching, medicine, charity work, politics, sales, entertainment, missionary work etc.

Type Two personalities are the helpers and givers in the Enneagram model who are willing to make sacrifices for others in their longing to feel loved and needed. In this chapter, we have examined the following -

- The characteristic features of Type Two personalities

- Famous Type Two personalities in history

- Typical roles that can be played by a Type Two personality

In the next chapter, we will examine the peculiar nature of Type Three personalities and how to recognise them. .

If you're enjoying this audiobook so far, I would appreciate it so much if you went to Audible and leave a short review.

Chapter 15: Type 1 And 2 Characteristics

Synopsis

The type ones are the strong perfectionists whether relating to self, home or society. Their constant desire is to improve things, make things better because things always never seem good enough to them. Their attention to detail is impeccable – often finding fault and fixing even the smallest things.

Helpers live to help others as far as their self worth is concerned. As long as they feel that they are in contribution to others, they feel they are worthy. They are typically selfless people and they believe that giving to others is their highest calling as they feel that love is the most important emotion in the world.

Type 1 Characteristics - Perfectionist, Reformer, Judge, Crusader or Critic

Highly principled and never compromising, they live by the book and follow all the rules or their code of conduct – they even expect others to do so as well. They also tend to be ambitious and to a point, like a workaholic. These people are truly serious people whose pursuit for perfection is often a blessing and a vice to people around them – especially when their primary fixation of resentment is manifested. It's no surprise that their holy idea is perfection. They are completely relentless at doing the thing right (sometimes at the expense of doing the right thing).

Their greatest fear is to succumb to the corruptness or evil desires of imperfection.

Cutting corners or taking the unethical way out is really painful to them.

They desire goodness, integrity and balance – because they often believe that being the good boy or good girl is the best way to go. Their biggest temptation is hypocrisy and hypercriticism. Because humans are imperfect beings, the constant pressure on perfection will lead them to manifest their hypocrisy as they cannot live to the high, lofty standards that they set for themselves and others. They are also extremely nit-picky because their greatest fear of being disappointed in others lead them to find fault with people's character.

Their greatest vice is anger and they express it by repressing it (convinced that the good boy or good girl never gets angry as it is 'improper'). Often, this catches them at the worst times and it leads to outbursts of extreme criticisms.

However, the type ones are at their best when they learn to accept the imperfections of themselves and others in order to take the right action.

Type ones with a wing of nine are often more peace loving with a subtle detached attitude while ones with a wing of two are generally warmer and has humanistic tendencies and sometimes extremely self-righteous tendencies.

Type 2 Characteristics - Giver, Caretaker, Helper, Nurturer, Advisor or Manipulator

These are the warmest, most helpful people around who will never forget your birthday (or feel really guilty when they do so...) and will go the extra mile to help one in need. An extrovert in nature, they work hard to relate and show love to all their friends and family. They live for appreciation and often fall into the trap of tending to the needs of others at the neglect of their own which often causes a problem. They are also highly manipulative especially when their primary fixation of flattery is manifested.

A helper's their holy idea is freedom. They love to express their love, care, feelings and emotions openly and happily with other people. Their greatest fear is that they are not worthy of the love of others. Their greatest difficulty is in defining their own needs because they tend to define their self worth through the eyes of others. If people think of them as a special friend, they will feel special – otherwise they will not have their own self worth.

They desire unconditional love which is often a two way thing. They like to give unconditional love and often expect unconditional love leading to doing things for others with strings attached.

Their biggest temptation is in being overtly or subtly manipulative. Because they are often doing it 'for their own good' it can sometimes lead to harm instead of goodness – hence the proverb, "The road to hell is paved with good intentions". In other words, the pursuit of 'helping' others can lead to detrimental results if the wrong action is taken.

Their greatest vice is vainglory because they often like being in the midst of praise of others (telling them how good they are for being so 'helpful').

However, the type ones are at their best when they learn to become truly altruistic – giving without conditions, loving unconditionally and sacrificing themselves for the greater good. Types twos with a wing of one are often highly principled, putting ethics before pride while twos with a wing of three are sociable, charming and heartfelt but susceptible to a double dose of vanity.

Chapter 16: Type Five– The Investigator

Fives are intense and intellectual. They can be perceptive and innovative. But, they can also be secretive and isolated.

Fives are insightful, curious, and alert. They enjoy solving mental puzzles. Fives are innovative and inventive, but they prefer to be independent. They tend to get lost in their mind contemplating solutions.

Despite becoming detached from society, Fives can be high-strung and intense. They develop problems with nihilism, eccentricity, and isolation. Many times, they focus too much energy on academic knowledge. They neglect developing social and practical skills.

In a positive light, Fives are visionary pioneers. They are considered "ahead of their time" because they have the ability to see the world and situations they encounter in a unique way. Fives are not turned on by the tried and true. Instead, they want to be the ones to discover uncharted territory, to be the first to know something. Many Fives will find one special niche they feel they can master.

Fives are motivated to learn as much as they can about the world around them.

They plan everything and use knowledge to protect themselves from setbacks.

Fives fear being useless, so they develop their mental capacity to devise enlightening solutions to complicated problems. They do not believe they have unique skills to offer. So, they use their research skills to learn new skills, so they have something to contribute to the world. They may use their knowledge and observations to invent something useful. Their contributions make them feel valuable as a person, but they want to be careful to wait until they know it works.

Fives are considered investigators because they strive to explore and learn as much as they can about how and why things are the way they are in natures. They even investigate their own feelings and imaginations. However, they are also the world's toughest skeptics. In an attempt to learn and explain as much as they can about the inner workings of life, they question everyone's theories until they are confident in their beliefs.

Type Fives with a Four-wing may be considered eccentric, while type Fives with a Six-wing are problem solvers.

Stress Point

When Type Fives are stressed, they may exhibit negative or unhealthy levels of development typically seen in Type Seven personalities.

These unhealthy traits include:

Bipolar

Erratic mood swings

Impulsive

Demanding

Uninhibited

Adventurous

Security Point

During times of growth Type Fives may exhibit positive or healthy levels of development typically seen in Type Eight personalities.

These healthy traits include:

Self-restrained

Merciful

Resourceful

Decisive

Authoritative

Self-confident

Self-sufficient

Levels of Development

Healthy:

Level 1

Visionary

Fives who are open-minded can make pioneering discoveries. Their capacity for new knowledge is limitless.

Level 2

Observationist

They are mentally alert and focused. Their curiosity leads them to more knowledge.

Level 3

Knowledge Master

They study their chosen field until they become "master of their domain."

Average:

Level 4

Studious

They become obsessed with making sure all their theories are accurate and fit together. Blueprints and models fill their offices.

Level 5

Detached

They become preoccupied with off-beat subjects that do not pertain to the practical world.

Level 6

Antagonistic

Fives become cynical and abrasive toward anyone who does not accept their views.

Unhealthy:

Level 7

Reclusive

They become fearful of aggression and rejection of their ideas, so they separate from social engagements.

Level 8

Phobic

They become obsessed with the dangers of the world and develop crazy phobias. If there's a one in a million chance being in danger by something they will fear it.

Level 9

Schizophrenic

By this point, Fives have had a devastating break from reality. They become deranged by their imaginations and abhor truth.

Chapter 17: Enneagram And Relationships With Other People

Successful self-development occurs when we understand our inner patterns, determine strengths and weaknesses, but it also depends on fostering healthy and strong relationships with other people. The Enneagram helps us improve relationships in different aspects of our life in more ways than one.

Relationships play a major role in our lives. From the very moment of birth, you are in a relationship (parents, siblings, other family members, friends, romantic parents etc.). Most people usually wonder what personality type suits them relationship-wise, but as mentioned earlier in the book, even though some types share similarities all of them are compatible with one another. The Enneagram is not like zodiac and doesn't help you improve relationships by suggesting you should engage with people who belong to the certain type.

When you understand your personality type it means you are aware of the inner patterns, motivations, desires, fears, virtues, and flaws. This means you understand where you're coming from. For example, a person who is Type Five understands what they seek in relationships with other people, but you also get an insight into how they perceive you.

By getting educated about other personality types, one finds it easier to understand their desires and what those people are looking for in different relationships. What can this teach you? Compromise! The key to a healthy relationship is a compromise. After all, the relationship isn't a dictatorship where one person is superior to the other and only they make all the choices. Both people in that relationship, romantic, platonic, family, should be equal and feel free to be open about their desires and what they expect from the other person. The Enneagram teaches you how to be confident, but still, accept other people's opinions and it's a great tool to improve every relationship in your life.

The opportunity to understand inner patterns of other people and compare them to yours helps you establish a deeper connection with others. This is the type of connection we are unable to achieve unless we understand ourselves and other people. It's like a domino effect because it's impossible to understand other people without knowing yourself. See, everything is connected, which is why the Enneagram is represented as a circle showing that although all nine personality types are different, they are strongly involved with one another.

Some people are open about their emotions, others aren't. Some of us are easily offended, but others are not. Plus, some people give love and want to be loved while others are confused and don't know how to express themselves the best way. All of us have different approaches to any type of relationship, but you always get puzzled. Why do people react/demand/feel certain things the way they do? Their Enneagram personality type explains it in detail. Learning how they react prevents you from taking them the wrong way or judging them.

How Enneagram improves relationships

As mentioned above, the Enneagram improves relationships in your life in many ways, including:

· Prevents over-thinking, which usually leads to misunderstanding and argument

· Increases empathy

· Decreases the risk of personalizing someone's behavior and misinterpreting it

· Ability to productively interact with any individual at home, work, or any other setting

· Creates strong, healthy relationships based on trust and honesty

· Opportunity to influence others constructively and vice versa, the

Enneagram shows that all types have a lot to learn from one another

· Helps understand who, in the work setting, is willing to grow as a person (ideal for team leaders)

· Helps you understand what employers, managers, and bosses want from people they work with and use that knowledge to further your career

Chapter 18: The Unbalanced Enneagram

The merits of harmony, and how things look when we lack it.

There are times when the master buries the bone deep.

There are other times when he **implies** he has buried the bone deep, causing all of his pupils to race around furiously digging holes, when actually, he left the bone right on the kitchen table.

One of the most essential principles in the Gurdjieff system is that an inner work must be a balanced work. Not only did he refer to his organization as the "Institute for Harmonious Development," but he also repeatedly emphasized the need for three centered work, a work in which all of the centers were balanced. And his protégés—most notably Jeanne de Salzmann—spoke about the need to balance inner work many times. For example, de Salzmann speaks in **The Reality Of Being** of getting the three centers to work at the same speed—something they don't do under ordinary circumstances, as Gurdjieff explained to Ouspensky in **In Search Of The Miraculous**.

Let's pause here for a moment and examine all of this information in the context of what Gurdjieff told Ouspensky about the wrong location of the second shock in the enneagram. The shock, he said, lawfully comes between the notes **si** and **do**. The diagram, however, "wrongly" locates it between **sol** and **la**.

Aside from his cryptic remarks about the fact that the wrong location indicated the type of work that was necessary for the second shock, Gurdjieff never elaborated on this. Longtime readers of my material may recall that in the past, I've offered a few possibilities for what he meant by that remark.

Here, we're going to offer what is perhaps a simpler and more obvious one. Take a look at the diagram of what the enneagram looks like when we locate the shock in the correct place.

Let's take a brief excursion into what symbols are for. Symbols are meant to represent abstractions of principles; they are not literal, but, literally, figurative interpretations of ideas. Symbols commonly undergo manipulation in order to more effectively express ideas that cannot be expressed literally.

The simplest possible explanation of what Gurdjieff was trying to get Ouspensky to understand when he talked about the shock being located in the "wrong" place on the diagram is that the type of work that is necessary to pass from **si** to **do** is a balanced work. The placement of the shock, in other words, creates a symmetrical and balanced diagram that properly represents the law of three functioning in a balanced way, instead of indicating one-sided or lopsided development of centers.

One sees the symbol is worthless if you draw it literally. It isn't even a symbol anymore: it's a mish-mosh which conveys gibberish instead of harmony. So there is no choice in the matter: in order to create an effective symbol of inner work that is harmoniously balanced, the shock must be located where it is. There are no special esoteric secrets connected to this; the esoteric secret is right here on the kitchen table, where no one notices it—exactly like every other real truth in life.

I suppose some may think it a bit sad to have to take this mysterious question and reduce it to such a simple point of view—especially those on an endless quest for secret magical knowledge—but it's actually not simple at all. The most essential problem we all have in our work is that we aren't well-balanced. We aren't harmonious. And we need to keep that question in front of us at all times. Seeing our lack is, in part, observing that imbalance up close and first-hand.

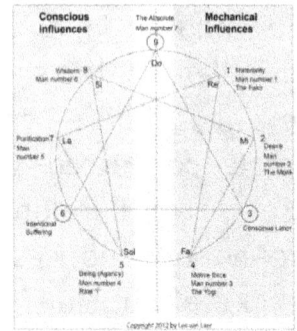

Conclusion

Abundance is related to the way we see our lives right now. So basically, it's down to seeing the glass half full or half empty. Are you a person who focuses instead on what you don't have? The rule of the Universe says you will get more of what you focus on. When you dwell on your mortgage, talk of hating your old car, focus on everything that's wrong in your relationship, and then you get more of this because it is so easy and strong that the Universe answers your thoughts.

Create a dream of what you want to attract in your mind. Keep it as vivid and dynamic as possible. Also, cut out magazine pictures. Write down how you want your life to live on a piece of paper. Don't include material possessions only. Write down how you'd like to feel like your normal day. You're employed, you're raising a family? Have you a lot of friends, live in the city or in the countryside? How much cash have you in the bank? And when you wake up, how do you feel? Build the vision — Essential-Write down what you want exactly as if you have it already. Remember, the Universe literally takes your thoughts. So, if you write,' I will live in a big country house,' it will always be a vision for you and stay in the future. In other words, in your present life, it will never materialize.

Be happy once you have developed your new dream of how you want to live your life. Be grateful for all you already have. Be grateful for the food you can consume, for your friends and family, for the TV, and even for the rusty old car on your drive, or your safety. Even if you don't feel good, your body keeps you alive. And thank you so much for that!

Thanksgiving is one of the main powers behind abundance. If you want to attract more to your life, be deeply grateful to have it already in your life. And by first class mail, the World will put on its skates and send more to you.

What you have in your life at the moment is a product of your past life. This can be a divisive assertion most people don't like listening to. It is far more appealing to the ego that other people are responsible for what we have, conditions beyond our control.

www.ingramcontent.com/pod-product-compliance
Lightning Source LLC
Chambersburg PA
CBHW072010070526
44583CB00015B/1422